14 Points

Successfully Involving Youth in Decision Making

14 Points: Successfully Involving Youth in Decision Making

For more information, contact:

Youth on Board
58 Day Street, Third Floor
P.O. Box 440322
Somerville, MA 02144

Phone: 617/923-9900 x1242
Fax: 617/623-4359
E-mail: YouthonBoard@aol.com
Web address: http://www.youthonboard.org

ISBN 0-9670649-0-2

Youth on Board is a project of YouthBuild USA.

Acknowledgements

These 14 points were drawn from the experiences and insights of a wide range of youth, youth allies, and youth organizations nation- and worldwide. This book has been shaped by many hands and continues to be a work in progress.

Conceived by:

Jenny Sazama
Karen S. Young

Managing Editor:

Kathryn Jones

Contributing Writers:

Michael Arnold
Tim Crellin
Mark Ferguson
Rachel Houghton
Kathryn Jones
Colleen Lannon

Jessica Liborio
Jeanie Ringelberg
Jenny Sazama
Maura Wolf
Karen S. Young

We'd like to thank the following colleagues who kindly reviewed and contributed to this book. Each of them offered valuable insights and thoughtful suggestions:

Shiuan Butler
Huong Hoang
Anne Hoover
Paul Millhouser

Dana Nelson
Suzette Rodriguez-O'Connor
Amy Weisenbach
Jennifer Wilding

Youth on Board is a project of YouthBuild USA. We thank them for their ongoing support.

To date, Youth on Board has received financial support from the W.K. Kellogg Foundation, Surdna Foundation Inc., the Edward Hazen Foundation, the Church Home Society, Fidelity Foundation, Levi Strauss Foundation, Haymarket People's Fund, the Orville W. Forte Foundation, Inc., the Susan A. and Donald P. Babson Charitable Foundation, The Boston Globe Foundation, The Boston Foundation, The Norman Foundation, The Hyams Foundation, The Salmon Foundation, The New England, The Reebok Foundation, Youth Service America, Fidelity Investments Charitable Gift Fund, Curet Fund, The Albert A. List Foundation, Laird, Norton Family Fund, Ruth and Lovett Peters Foundation, Oak Lodge Foundation, and our generous individual donors. Their financial assistance makes this and all other Youth on Board projects possible.

14 Points:
Successfully Involving Youth in Decision Making

Table of Contents

Acknowledgments iii

Introduction vii

Point 1: Know Why You Want to Involve Young People 1

Point 2: Conduct an Organizational Assessment 15

Point 3: Determine Your Model for Youth Involvement 29

Point 4: Identify Organizational Barriers 41

Point 5: Overcome Attitudinal Barriers 55

Point 6: Address Legal Issues 71

Point 7: Recruit Young People. 87

Point 8: Create a Strong Orientation Process 107

Point 9: Train Young People for Their Roles. 123

Point 10: Conduct Intergenerational Training 137

Point 11: Make Meetings Work 161

Point 12: Develop a Mentoring Plan. 177

Point 13: Build Youth/Adult Relationships 187

Point 14: Create Support Networks. 199

Resource Directory 215

Introduction

Today's young people and their allies are living during a precarious time in history. On the one hand, the distance between youth and adults seems to be growing—as many as 2,000 young people nationwide quit school each day, and numerous others act out their frustration through violence, crime, and drug abuse. The social problems of poverty, early pregnancy, school violence, racism, and classism feed into the frustration that young people feel, causing them to drop out of society at an alarming rate. This leaves many adults asking why, and searching for causes in music, television and movies, style of dress, and video games, rather than looking at the root of the problem— too many young people have no vested interest in their future, and no feelings of ownership of their communities.

On the other hand, adult professionals are increasingly looking at innovative ways to nurture and develop strong young people, from educational reform to social programs. And, adults are turning to young people themselves for ideas and solutions. Listening to young people and including them in the decisions and organizations that affect their lives is part of a nationwide movement that reflects a growing awareness that young people's voices are missing in our communities, schools, and churches. Youth on Board has been at the forefront of this movement and, as more people join, we look with excitement to what the future brings.

The decisions we make as adult allies—what we do for, with, and about youth—is crucial to the future of young people and of society as a whole.

Therefore, the decisions we make as adult allies—what we do for, with, and about youth—is crucial to the future of young people and of society as a whole. Typically and traditionally in many cultures, young people have been excluded from efforts to rebuild their communities. This marginalization of our youth not only harms them and endangers our future, but it also cheats the world of a valuable resource. If we are to function effectively as local and even global communities, then we must incorporate all significant voices. Enduring, positive community renewal is possible only if *all* members are involved and feel ownership. Negative attitudes about young people can and must be broken down—and Youth on Board firmly believes this goal is possible.

14 Points: Successfully Involving Youth in Decision Making is the foundation on which all other Youth on Board materials are built as we work to help dismantle the barriers that divide young people from adults, from their peers, and from their communities. This book focuses on a logical starting point—including young people as equal partners in the decision-making processes of youth-centered organizations, churches, city councils, school committees, tribal councils, etc. It is a step-by-step manual that includes both the philosophy behind and an action plan for this work. Though it is designed for board members, corporate executives, parents, community partners, teachers, and others who work with youth and want to develop governing structures that work more effectively, it can be appreciated by and useful to people of any age.

Youth on Board's mission is to revolutionize the role of young people in society by: changing attitudes and strengthening relationships among youth, and between young people and adults; preparing young people to be leaders and decision makers in all aspects of their lives; and ensuring that policies, practices, and laws reflect young people's role as full and valued members of their communities. We are unique in that we don't just help build skills, we also

The marginalization of our youth not only harms them and endangers our future, but it also cheats the world of a valuable resource.

help build mutually respectful relationships between young people and adults. We believe that one of the crucial issues for community development anywhere is to create leaders at the fastest possible rate, at all levels of the community—leaders who are skilled, ethical, effective, and unifying. Young people are most eager to play a leadership role in these efforts.

What do we mean by "young people"?

At first glance, this question is not difficult to answer: young people are "kids" or "children," perhaps "someone my age" or "anyone younger than myself." But consider how varying organizations and initiatives use different definitions for young people, youth, and young adults. Some call anyone under age 30 a young person. Others refer to people ages 13-19 as teens. Many programs don't even make age distinctions, calling everyone younger than the person speaking "kids."

This distinction may seem insignificant, but the failure to recognize it has serious implications for youth involvement. Though governing structures are reserving positions for "young people" with more frequency, all too often these well-intentioned organizations select someone who is older—a local graduate student or a parent in their mid-20s. It is not wrong to include these people, but our failure to accurately identify "young people" prevents us from actively seeking out those youth whose voices are not being heard—those who are too young to vote or seek political office—and bring them into decision-making processes. People in their teens and those in their 20s lead very different lives.

To eliminate this kind of confusion, we divide "youth" into two separate categories:

Young people are those under 20 years of age. This category includes toddlers, children, and teens. It is understood, of course, that children who are three years old experience the world very differently than those who are six, and then again from those who are 16. People of all these ages, however, are united in that they are socially and legally restricted because of their age.

Young adults range from 21 to 30 years of age. It is clear that 21 is not the age that actually represents the transition point into adulthood for all people. We choose 21 as the age of induction to young adulthood because legal rights are conferred at this age in many societies worldwide. Young adults are in a difficult spot—they are too old to be "protected" by adults, and still too young to know all about what it means to be an adult, and as such they may not be afforded the same respect as older adults.

Getting the most from this book

This book is laid out in a step-by-step fashion, from an explanation of why young people should be involved in governance (*Point 1: Know Why You Want to Involve Young People*), to key steps of the process, such as recruiting (*Point 7: Recruit Young People*) and mentoring (*Point 12: Develop a Mentoring Plan*), to a discussion of ways to support yourself and others as you move forward (*Point 14: Create Support Networks*). If you are currently involved in a youth leadership program, we recommend that you first scan the chapter title pages to see which areas are most relevant to your current situation. Or, if you know you want to involve youth but need direction, we suggest you begin with the organizational assessment (*Point 2: Conduct an Organizational Assessment*). If you are convincing others that youth in governance is a good idea, or need further convincing yourself, then it's best to start at the beginning. It can be helpful to discuss the book with someone else as you are reading it. However you approach it, jot down questions and ideas that you want to keep in mind. At the end of each point, you'll find worksheets that you can use for yourself and for members of your governing body. These worksheets will help you think through the issues and challenges and create solutions for them. We encourage you to photocopy these worksheets (see page *ii* for our entire photocopy policy) and work through them with members of your organization.

Let's get started!

By purchasing this book, you have already made a positive step toward a future in which barriers between young people and adults no longer exist. You know that it's time to stop dreaming about youth inclusion and start assisting young people as they work to make decisions that are of the utmost importance to them and future generations. It can happen, and it will happen, because it has to happen—hopelessness is getting old, and there is no need for us to throw up our hands in exasperation and defeat. So, let's get to work!

POINT NUMBER 1

Know Why You Want to Involve Young People

This chapter discusses several common motivations for involving young people on councils, task forces, boards, church vestries, etc., and invites readers to reflect on their own interests and goals.

*I*n Marquette, MI, police and young people were at a stand-off. Many townspeople were upset that young people were "taking over" downtown streets to skateboard. The young people were angry because the police were moving them from the one hangout in town where they felt they had the right to be. The Marquette City Commission and young people decided to set up a youth advisory board to help solve the problem and give adults and youth a forum to talk. Little did both sides know what was about to emerge: a harmonious joint effort by police officers and skateboarders to plan and build a skateboard park.

This story, which shows what can happen when young people and adults work together on equal ground, illustrates one of the thousands of reasons why it makes sense to involve young people in governance roles. There are countless examples that youth involvement leads to innovative solutions, stronger communities, and increased self-esteem among young people who feel supported by adults, rather than feeling ruled by them.

If you are reading this manual, it's likely that you already believe in youth involvement. Or perhaps you know it's important, but need a little more information to help convince others that creating a youth council, electing a young person to a board, or setting up a youth policy committee makes sense. Use this chapter to strengthen your own beliefs and to challenge others to get on board.

Who Benefits?

People sometimes ask, "Does anyone but young people benefit from youth empowerment?" At Youth on Board, we believe that *everyone* does. Society needs young people to value their own endless potential. Rather than producing generations of apathetic and disenfranchised youth, society would do well to involve young people in decision making. By becoming actively involved in leadership roles, young people are encouraged to take ownership of their communities. This leads to increased self-confidence and feelings of success, which in turn leads youth away from crime, drugs, and other self-destructive activities.

Above and beyond the impact on the young people themselves, involving youth in a nonprofit or governing structure can revitalize a group. Young people bring energy and a fresh perspective, often catalyzing other group members to rethink their priorities, their commitment, and the invisible barriers that have kept them from moving forward. In addition, most nonprofits acknowledge that having people whom their services or policies directly affect involved in the governance of their organizations helps to keep them focused on their mission. For example, it is less likely that a community center with young people on its board would build a new youth wing that young people won't want to use. Increased input and investment usually pays off in both the short and the long term.

Another reason why an organization might be interested in involving young people in their governance is to develop new leadership and support for the future. For example, if a community foundation wants to cultivate young donors, it would be wise to recruit young people for its board. By the time those young people become adults, they will be well informed about the importance and impact of that institution, and thus more likely to support it with their time and money.

There are countless other reasons to involve young people in governance. The important step is to define your own motives. Are you looking to spice up a boring community group? Do you have a commitment to giving stakeholders and constituents representation on an advisory board? Do you think having youth representation will

Involving youth in a nonprofit or governing structure can revitalize a group.

help attract funders? Being clear about your own motives will guide your efforts and inspire others to trust you, because they will know where you are coming from.

Use the following text to introduce the concept of youth governance to others. Have individual conversations with people about the pros and cons of increased youth involvement. Use the worksheet at the end of this chapter in a full group meeting to consider the issues for your board or governing council. Take steps *now* to get youth involved in your organization—everyone will benefit from the experience.

Common Motivations for Inviting Young People to the Table[1]

It's a diversity issue

Even though they may not have years of formal experience, youth offer intelligence, creative thinking, and a valuable outlook on the world that is seldom introduced into the governance of organizations. While age diversity might not show up on a typical diversity chart, it is a critical element for boards that want to embrace many voices and perspectives.

But it is important to remember that there is no "stock" young person. Their opinions and ideas are as varied as those of any other group. Age is only one shaping force in their lives. Like the rest of us, young people's outlooks are deeply affected by their personal experiences; their racial, economic, religious, and sexual identities; and their individual personalities.

It's a democracy issue

To make a democracy work, all people need to be heard. This

[1] Some of the ideas in this text were taken from a speech given by Amy Weisenbach of the National 4-H Council at the 1998 National Assembly Forum.

includes the voices of young people. We need to hear their views, ideas, and passions. We also need to act on their ideas, so that democracy continues to thrive in future generations.

It's a bottom-line issue

Quite simply, young people are uniquely qualified to say what works for young people. By relying on young decision makers to provide personal insights, talk with friends, and organize youth focus groups, organizations can save time and money by catching decisions that might not work well with young people *before* they are enacted and fail.

It's a civil rights issue

Nowhere in the U.S. Declaration of Independence is there a stipulation concerning age. "*All* men are created equal," *all* are entitled to "certain unalienable rights." So why is it that, in this country, decisions that affect a significant segment of the population are made by others? In far too many situations, young people are not being heard. Their rights are being disregarded or violated, and adults do not seem to hear or care about it. This needs to change. Our communities need to allow young people's concerns to be heard and taken seriously. They have the same right as adults to voice their fears, hopes, and ideas.

It's a youth development issue

Being a leader can change the life of a young person. Leadership helps young people develop confidence in their opinions and their ideas. For many young people, being a leader will mark the first time that their ideas have been instrumental in real decision making. In addition to fostering confidence, participating as a leader can introduce youth to a range of other skills—public speaking, budgeting, leading projects and committees, and networking, to name a few.

By creating visible youth decision-making positions, you can enhance the self-esteem of young people in your organization and throughout your community. It bolsters *all* young people's self-confidence to see their peers being taken seriously, and having youth leaders will generate a positive reputation for your organization or initiative.

It's a long-term growth issue

Educating youth about the ideals of the nonprofit sector and community service can plant the seeds of social responsibility in their heads. Youth, in turn, can provide a new generation of leadership. Some organizations realize that everyone on staff and in decision-making positions is getting older. Adding young people to the governance of an aging organization can usher in a new generation of leadership.

It's an organizational culture issue

Youth can enliven the atmosphere of your organization. Young people bring energy and enthusiasm to their work. They often remind us that work and fun are not mutually exclusive. In addition, most organizations incorporate more interactive work processes when they involve youth. Techniques like small group discussions or brainstorming encourage teamwork and foster better communication by giving people a chance to be heard. Everyone, regardless of age, is at their best and brightest when they are comfortable expressing themselves.

It's a community outreach issue

Young people bring an entirely new community of contacts to your organization. If young people are out front and vocal about your committee or organization, other young people will be drawn to find out about what you are doing. Youth are able to plug into the world of their peers in ways that adults, as outsiders, simply cannot. Keep in mind that word-of-mouth advertising is *extremely* effective

Young people bring energy and enthusiasm to their work. They often remind us that work and fun are not mutually exclusive.

among young people. By adding youth to your decision-making body, you are expanding your circle of clients, constituents, or consumers, and adding to their understanding of your group.

It's an integrity issue

It is important for any organization to involve its constituents. Just as it would not make sense for the NAACP (National Association for the Advancement of Colored People) to be run exclusively by white people, it does not make sense for youth-serving organizations to be run exclusively by adults.

Even as sensible as this sounds, many nonprofits do not involve young people, even as they purportedly strive to include all of their constituents. In its 1997 study, "A Snapshot of America's Nonprofit Boards," the National Center for Nonprofit Boards profiled 1,028 boards from nonprofits of varying sizes, locations, and mission areas. While there was no count of youth-serving organizations, 12 percent of these nonprofits identified their mission area as education, and it is reasonable to infer that organizations from other mission areas (like health and human services) also have youth constituents.

Of the board members behind these 1,028 organizations, 23 percent were chosen because of their status as clients and consumers. Only three percent of the members, however, were under the age of 30. Although the survey demonstrates these organizations' commitment to include clients and consumers in governance, young people, who we can assume make up a large portion of their clients and consumers, are still severely underrepresented.

Checking Your Interests

What does youth involvement mean to you and your organization? In 1975, the National Commission on Resources for Youth defined the term as follows:

Youth participation is the involving of youth in responsible, challenging action that meets genuine needs, with opportunities for planning and/or decision-making affecting others in an activity whose impact or consequence is extended to others—i.e., outside or beyond the youth participants themselves. Other desirable features of youth participation are provision for critical reflection on the participatory activity and the opportunity for group effort toward a common goal.

For some organizations, youth involvement will mean having a few young board members, while for others it may take the form of a youth advisory group or hiring youth staff. A myriad of ways to involve young people, including those listed below, are covered in *Point 3: Determine Your Model for Youth Involvement*. Some examples are:

- Board members
- Staff members
- Youth advisory group members
- Special assistants for a project or presentation
- Volunteers
- Interns

Developing Clear Goals and Objectives

If you ask five different people what their favorite ice cream store is, you'll probably get five different answers. Why? Because each person has different expectations for what makes a "great" shop. Is it a place where people love to hang out? Or is it the place with the most flavor selections? Success in finding the right place has everything to do with articulating your expectations.

As it is with ice cream, so it is with youth involvement. When thinking about what a successful youth involvement strategy might look like, carefully consider your expectations and what outcomes you hope to achieve. Use the questions on the worksheet at the end of this chapter to develop a clear set of goals and objectives in the area of youth involvement.

When doing so, consider your vision for youth involvement, your concerns, and your organization's past history with similar efforts.

Defining objectives

Defining objectives is a way to set up a benchmark for your group or organization, and a way to realistically reach your goal(s). While you will also want to have larger goals to keep you focused in the right direction, objectives will lead the way. They should be specific, tangible, and attainable. Here are some sample objectives, taken from the New York Youth Council's publication *Youth Adult Partnership* :

- The Board of Directors of the ABC organization will be restructured to ensure that one-tenth of its members are youth.

- By next fall, the Executive Director will recruit, screen, and select 10 youth (who have previously received our services) for employment in our organization.

- Within three months, a Youth Outreach Committee will be operating and will have increased by 30 percent the number of 16- to 19-year-olds coming to our center.

- By involving youth in community events, the Downtown Business Commission will reduce vandalism by 50 percent in the business district over the next year.

- Within one year, 75 percent of the youth involved with our board will have developed knowledge and skills related to running an organization.

Note that each of these objectives is tied to dates and measurable outcomes. At the end of the time period, the group can look back and see if it has achieved its objectives.

What are your goals and objectives? What is your process for defining them?

1

STORIES FROM THE STREET

◆ When Marie Celestin completed Youth on Board's Springboard Training Institute, she became a board co-chair for the Massachusetts Youth Service Alliance, and established the G.I.R.L.S.[2] (Growing Individuals Reacting to Life's Struggles) Conference. This annual girl-led, girl-run event in the Boston area provides a forum for girls to speak out and to be heard on various social, economic, and educational issues.

◆ When the Promise Project[3]—a project of the YMCA of Kansas City, MO—started, one young person was included on the advisory board. They soon realized that one young person was not enough representation, and the board increased the number of young people to three. Currently, the Promise Project is in the process of creating a policy that mandates that 50 percent of advisory board members be under the age of 21.

◆ Sisters Empowering Sisters (SES), the Girl's Advisory Group of the Girl's Best Friend Foundation[4] (GBF), was started in 1998 to bring girls' voices into the Foundation. As a girl-directed, girl-driven project, SES brings the voices of girls to the GBF Foundation by researching the experiences and challenges that girls in the Chicago-area face, evaluating grant applications from other girl-directed groups, deliberating and deciding on grants, and sharing information and experiences with others interested in the lives of girls.

[2] G.I.R.L.S. c/o Patriots' Trail Girl Scouts, 95 Berkeley Street, Boston, MA 02116. Phone: 617/482-1078

[3] See the *Resource Directory,* located at the end of this book, for Promise Project contact information.

[4] Girl's Best Friend Foundation, 900 N. Franklin, Suite 608, Chicago, IL 60610. Phone: 312/266-2842.

Developing Clear Goals and Objectives

Use this worksheet to help you think about what your goals and objectives are for youth involvement. Review the examples of expectations and objectives below. Then lead participants in the guided visioning session. Finally, fill out the chart together as a group.

Group visioning: Where are you going?

Have everyone pair off and discuss what they envision would be the best possible youth/adult partnership for the group. To make it more tangible, imagine yourselves sitting in a meeting—who is there, what is the agenda, and what are the rules of the meeting? At the end of the meeting, what is happening? Who is talking to whom and what are they saying?

After several minutes, ask everyone to reconvene as a group and share their ideas. Use the ideas generated as a backdrop for a focused discussion about your organization's expectations and objectives in its strategy to involve youth.

Discussion questions

Now that you have a good idea of what you're looking for, it will be easier to create goals and objectives specific to your organization. As a group, discuss the following questions before you make your list:

• What makes you nervous or apprehensive about involving youth?

• Have you had positive experiences involving young people in other organizations?

• Have you had negative experiences involving young people in other organizations?

• What is the history of this organization's involvement of young people?

• Do you have a target group of youth in mind?

• What are the qualifications, skills, interests, or commitment levels of the young people you want to involve?

• Are you willing to commit time, money, or other tangibles to this effort?

• If there is likely to be a barrier or a pitfall to this effort, what might it be?

• Where will you need help?

It's time to create your own list of expectations and objectives. Be as specific as possible, looking back to the section of example objectives as needed.

Example:

Goal: To create a youth policy committee that advises the city council on key program and policy directions.

Objectives: 1. Recruit a diverse group of youth for the committee by the spring.

                2. Conduct an orientation and training program during the summer.

                3. Give a city councilor's office the responsibility of hosting regular meetings with the youth policy committee and providing the full city council with updates and recommendations on an ongoing basis.

Develop your own list

Goal #1_____

Objectives _____

_____

_____

_____

Goal #2_____

Objectives: _____

_____

_____

_____

Goal #3_____

Objectives: _____

_____

_____

_____

**POINT
NUMBER**

Conduct an Organizational Assessment

This chapter outlines a process to help your group assess how ready you are to involve young people in governance positions. The organizational assessment is useful for all organizations, no matter where they are in the youth involvement process.

N o matter how ready you are to involve young people in leadership positions, an organizational assessment can help you. The purpose of conducting an organizational assessment is to determine what is needed for youth to be successfully integrated into your governance structure. It is not a fail-safe mechanism, of course, but it is one of the best ways to promote success. Are you already strong in most areas related to supporting youth involvement? The assessment can offer suggestions for different approaches or improvements. Do you have specific areas for major growth? The assessment can help you identify specific changes that should be made.

A major part of conducting an assessment is enlisting support for your cause. While your group may be personally committed to involving youth in governance, it is crucial that youth also have the support of your entire organization and the structures in place to assist them. Assembling a board committee to research and help prepare for youth involvement can be an excellent way to invest your board in this idea. You can also include individual conversations with all board members to make sure they understand and support youth involvement. And, finally, your staff can be the cornerstone that makes this project work. In many organizations, staff members support new young members by helping them prepare for meetings or by providing transportation. This kind of effort can be a great way to foster a deeper relationship between your staff, board, and young people.

As you know, adding young people to your group may be viewed as a radical change by the adults in your organization. On the other hand, there may be others who are ready to add young decision makers to the mix right away. Once you know where everyone stands, you can be more strategic about how to proceed.

Assembling a board committee to research and help prepare for youth involvement can be an excellent way to invest your board in this idea.

Planning Your Strategy:
Immediate or Gradual Change?

There once was a church that had two ministers in the span of two years. The first minister wanted to feel more like a part of the congregation when he gave his sermons. So one day, he decided to move the pulpit to the same level as the parishioners. He got out his hammer and nails, uprooted the pulpit, and moved it. Surveying his handiwork, he felt sure the people would appreciate his efforts. The reaction on Sunday surprised him. Some people were delighted with the new change, while others were infuriated. At a special meeting of the church council, church leaders had a heated discussion about this radical shift. By the end of the meeting, they had full agreement that this was clearly not the minister for this church, and they asked him to leave.

A few months later, another minister arrived at the same church. He greeted the parishioners and began getting to know them and their families. He, too, believed that the pulpit should be placed at the same level as the people. He wanted parishioners to see him as one of them.

When he brought the idea up at a council meeting, he was regaled with many stories about the previous minister's miserable failure. He listened intently to the concerns and worries. The following week, he got out his hammer and nails. He uprooted the pulpit and moved it— one inch closer to the people. That Sunday he preached as usual and no one seemed to notice the change. The next week he moved the pulpit again—one more inch forward. Again, no one noticed. By the end of the year, he was right down with the people. The change had happened so gradually, people were only vaguely aware that things were different. What they did notice was how great his sermons were, and how much a part of the congregation he seemed.

Like the second minister, one of the most important things you can do before including young people in the decision-making process of your organization is to gain a clear sense of how fast your organization is willing to change.

As much as you may want change to happen smoothly, it is inevitable that you will hit barriers in your quest to involve youth. Moving through or over these barriers will test your resolve, and that of the individuals on your council and on your staff. Don't give up. With support from everyone, these obstacles will be easier to face.

We encourage you to move forward proactively to ensure the successful inclusion of youth in your group. By conducting an organizational assessment and defining areas where you want to focus and grow, you can address many of the issues that other groups face only after a conflict has emerged.

Conducting an Organizational Assessment

The steps listed below describe in detail each of the areas covered by the assessment. Once you have reviewed and evaluated your organization according to these steps, engage others in the process. Set aside a meeting where your group can fill out the organizational assessment worksheet at the end of this chapter, and then discuss the outcomes.

Step 1: Structure

Recruitment, selection, and retention

There are many strategies for recruitment, selection, and retention (see *Point 7: Recruit Young People*). The amount of energy you put into them will be reflected in the caliber, diversity, and commitment of the young people (and adults) you recruit. In fact, you should have the same recruitment criteria for youth and adults. If you do a poor job in the area of recruitment and selection, don't be surprised if you later struggle with retention problems.

Also, use the recruitment process to educate those your organization serves about the purpose of the governing body, and the importance of getting young people involved. Once your constituency realizes

The amount of energy you put into recruitment strategies will be reflected in the caliber, diversity, and commitment of the young people you recruit.

what your board or council is trying to accomplish, they may serve as effective recruiters for new youth board members.

Roles and responsibilities

Just as with anyone, if young people are playing a central role in your group, they are likely to know it and, in return, show higher commitment to the effort. If young people are involved in decision making in all areas of the group, not just in issues directly related to young people, it is a sign that you place a high value on young people's ideas and advice, regardless of the content.

Process

A strong commitment to young people means that a group is willing to shift some of the ways it does business to involve them more fully. One way this occurs is in the process of meetings. Do your meetings provide opportunities for everyone to share their thoughts? Are there warm-up exercises to get people loosened up and ready to participate? These and other strategies (refer to *Point 11: Make Meetings Work*) can have a big impact on the success of your efforts, making meeting better for all involved.

Bylaws and terms

One area that many organizations have not addressed is a change in their bylaws to ensure youth involvement in the years to come. Bylaws are a set of rules that an organization adopts to govern its members and regulate its affairs. Not all governing bodies have bylaws, but most boards of directors do. As with all changes to your bylaws, you should secure legal counsel before you write in a permanent role for young people (see the "Bylaws" section in *Point 4: Identify Organizational Barriers* for a further explanation and examples).

Terms of serving in a leadership capacity in your organization should be spelled out specifically for all new members, youth and adult. Matters such as how long members must serve, age requirements, and time and travel requirements should all be specified.

One area that many organizations have not addressed is a change in their bylaws to ensure youth involvement in the years to come.

Step 2: Support

Financial support

Young people often face financial issues that many adults don't think much about. For instance, some young people will not even apply for your council position if they know they will have to incur a number of out-of-pocket expenses. Even when groups reimburse young people, financial issues remain a barrier because youth often don't have money up front. Think about the following suggestions:

• **Pay young people's expenses in advance rather than reimburse them.** While many groups expect members to front money for expenses like transportation, postage, and photocopies, young people seldom have the financial resources to absorb even reimbursed expenses.

• **Create a policy to compensate young people for lost wages if they must miss work for meetings.** Adults with salaried positions often have more time flexibility than young people, who may lose wages if they have to take time off from work to fulfill their responsibilities.

• **Provide funding or assistance to support care for children of young parents.** There are many young parents, and parents in general, who can't afford a babysitter but have huge contributions to make in governance environments. Supporting serious needs like these can attract youth who might otherwise shy away from involvement. Such funding can also be a good resource for all parents on your board.

General support

Young people may need support around specific circumstances in their lives, such as help with transportation to and from meetings. Establishing a carpool plan for young members can help attendance and ensure safe transport. Also consider these tips:

• **Have tutors or other people available who can assist young people with schoolwork before or after meetings.** This kind of exceptional consideration will make it clear to youth that you are committed to their success, both inside and outside your organization.

- **Provide snacks for people who come directly from school or work.** We all know how uncomfortable it is to be stuck in a meeting with a rumbling stomach. Making sure basic human needs are met will invariably make for a better meeting.

- **Provide young people with information about nonprofits and being effective decision makers.** Refer to *Point 9: Train Young People for Their Roles,* for a list of training topics. Youth on Board conducts thorough training sessions for young people at all levels of governance involvement.

Emotional support

Emotional support can take the form of encouraging words to young people, letting them know that their work is important and that they should stay involved. Or, it may be important to create a time and space where it's safe for young people to share their thoughts freely, especially when someone feels that she or he is not being heard. For more emotional support ideas, see *Point 13: Build Youth/Adult Relationships*.

Personal support

One of the most valuable investments you can make to ensure success is to create structures that support young people on a personal level. Establishing a mentoring system that matches new committee or board members with old ones can have a tremendous impact. Young people can also benefit from time with each other, when they can share their experiences and offer support to each other. Other ways of providing strong personal support for young people are to:

- **Have someone make reminder phone calls to young people before each meeting.** Since young people have are not usually accustomed to keeping datebooks and have irregular schedules that they sometimes do not directly control, it can be invaluable to remind them of upcoming meetings. This is an excellent way to let youth know that they are needed at each meeting, and that they will be missed if they do not attend. A simple phone call may make the difference in your young members' attendance.

• **Have an adult authority who can help explain meetings to concerned parents.** It is important to remember that even very independent young people are answerable to their families. Involving parents and other concerned adults in this experience can actually strengthen an organization's community ties. Additionally, parents can be excellent allies as we all work to assist young people in having their lives go well.

Step 3: Attitude

Your group might have all the right structures and policies in place, but have unspoken attitudes and assumptions about young people that will limit their effectiveness. It is critical that your group think hard about why it wants to involve young people in governance and that a good portion of the group is supportive before you move forward. There must be an attitude of respect for each person's intelligence and capability, and a belief that young people can learn to handle the decisions and work that comes their way.

Similarly, young people must have a positive attitude in order for their presence to be effective. Young people can fall into the trap of thinking that they have nothing to say and thus nothing to contribute, or that adults won't listen if they do speak up. Enthusiasm for the work and for the cause is key to a young person's success in any governance structure. Just filling a chair won't do anyone any good.

Step 4: Behavior

Adult behavior

If adults are already building strong relationships with young people, supporting their involvement, and really listening to what they have to say, then you're heading in the right direction. In short, one's behavior is a reflection of one's attitude. You can learn a lot about

It is critical that your group think hard about why it wants to involve young people in governance.

your organization's readiness for greater youth governance by watching how adults interact with young people.

Youth behavior

You can also learn a lot about an organization's readiness to involve youth by watching the young people involved. In an organization that takes young people seriously, you will see young people taking on leadership positions, asking to serve on committees, sharing their opinions, and questioning/challenging behaviors that they see as patronizing.

Step 5: Training

Take a look at the support systems you have in place to ensure a smoothly working board. A strong orientation and training plan can be key to young people's successful involvement. Many times, young people come into their role as board members feeling somewhat insecure about their skill level and expertise. Information about topics such as budgets, meeting protocol, agendas, and Robert's Rules can help young people feel confident in their role. It is also important for adults to participate in training geared toward helping them develop communication and listening skills specific to working with young people in governance situations.

A strong orientation and training plan can be key to young people's successful involvement.

2

Though National 4-H Council[1], with its youth-based mission, has involved young people as consultants, advisors, committee and task force members, youth were left out of one vital role—decision making in its governance structure. National 4-H Council is a private partner of the nationwide 4-H youth program, which serves more than six million young people nationwide.

A 1990 marketing research study of why youth left 4-H found that the young people were "tired of being in an organization run by adults who thought they knew what was best for kids." Further study led the Council to change its mission in 1994. Today, the mission is "to be an uncommon youth development organization fostering innovation and shared learning for youth workers and young leaders."

The idea of including youth on the Council board at the highest level of decision making initially met with resistance. Adult members were accostomed to making decisions for youth, not with them. So, even when two young leaders joined the board with full voting privileges in 1992, things did not change immediately. The youth didn't feel comfortable talking at the board meetings. They were given no orientation, and did not know what it meant to serve on a board. Similarly, no one prepared Council members for the challenges of integrating young people into the boardroom. Before long, the youth decided to take action to make things easier for future board members. Drawing on the resources of Youth on Board, Council staff created an orientation protocol and materials for all future National 4-H Council board members—both youth and adults.

But this was only the beginning. In 1998, young board member Amy Weisenbach appealed to the board to add more young people to the Council. She showed them a video featuring interviews with trustees of other boards that shared power with youth. As a result, National 4-H Council's board voted to expand to include 10 young people ranging in age from 12 to 22.

At 4-H, youth took a stand, and the organization has benefited from their unique insights. As a result, National 4-H Council is fulfilling its own mission—involving youth in decision making at every level of its organization. The Council now raves about its partnership model.

---

[1] See the *Resource Directory*, located at the end of this book, for National 4-H Council contact information.

Organizational Assessment Checklist

Using this checklist

This tool is to be used as a guide to highlight issues that may help or hinder the participation of young people. Assessing your organization's readiness to involve youth as decision makers is an excellent way to help everyone understand the task at hand and gauge their commitment to this initiative. Please note that we are not suggesting that every organization meet all of these criteria.

KEY

Yes =   We do this already, and don't need to take further action
N/A =   This is not applicable to us
To consider =   We want to move forward in this area or have questions about whether this applies to us

Step 1: Structure

Yes	N/A	To consider	
			Recruitment, Selection, and Retention
☐	☐	☐	When recruiting members, do you use methods that will attract a diverse group of young people?
☐	☐	☐	Do you use your recruitment process to educate your constituency about the governance body and the importance of young people being involved?
☐	☐	☐	Have you outlined recruitment criteria for new members (e.g., motivation for the cause, readiness for the environment, etc.)?
☐	☐	☐	Is recruitment criteria the same for adult new members as it is for young new members?
☐	☐	☐	Is there a replacement system if a young person's term ends early (e.g., due to relocation or going to college)?
☐	☐	☐	Do you have a system in place for youth members to train new youth members?
			Roles and Responsibilities
☐	☐	☐	Are young people included in visible leadership positions?
☐	☐	☐	Are young people involved in all issues, not just those affecting their age group?
			Process
☐	☐	☐	Do you start meetings with warm-up exercises or frequently split into small groups?
☐	☐	☐	Is there time for all members to speak at meetings?
			Bylaws and Terms
☐	☐	☐	Have you amended bylaws or created policies stating that young people will be a permanent part of governing your organization?

Yes	N/A	To consider	
☐	☐	☐	Do you have at least two young members on your governing body or, alternatively, a solid youth advisory group?
☐	☐	☐	Are young people's terms of office similar or equal to those of adults?
☐	☐	☐	Do young people have equal voting status on your board, or does your youth advisory group substantially influence governance of the organization?

Step 2: Support

Financial

☐	☐	☐	Are young people's expenses (e.g., transportation to meetings) paid for in advance as opposed to being reimbursed ?
☐	☐	☐	Do young people have access to the resources needed to participate in your group's work (e.g., long distance phone cards, faxes, overnight mail, computers, and copy machines)?

General/Emotional/Personal

☐	☐	☐	Is there a mentor or buddy system in place?
☐	☐	☐	Is staff available /willing to support youth members (e.g., preparation, transportation for meetings, etc.)?
☐	☐	☐	Is there informal time for networking with other members?
☐	☐	☐	Are retreats held to build cohesion in the group?
☐	☐	☐	Is there contact between young members and the executive director or chair before and/or after meetings?
☐	☐	☐	Do young people keep in touch with their peers about their governance role?
☐	☐	☐	Is an adult of authority available to explain commitments to concerned parents?
☐	☐	☐	Is there a place where young people can voice their concerns outside of a meeting setting?

Step 3: Attitude

☐	☐	☐	Is your group clear about why you are involving young people in governance?
☐	☐	☐	Is some consideration given for conflicts between board commitments and young people's participation in school activities? (Work meetings are often an acceptable reason for adults to miss meetings. Is a basketball game given the same consideration?)
☐	☐	☐	Does the group understand that youth members do not represent the voice of all young people?
☐	☐	☐	Do the young people on your board seem enthusiastic about and interested in the group's tasks?
☐	☐	☐	Do young group members ask questions and respectfully acknowledge that they can learn a lot from adult board members?

Step 4: Behavior

Yes	N/A	To consider	
			Adult behavior
☐	☐	☐	Do you continually ask young people how you can better work together, and do you take their recommendations seriously?
☐	☐	☐	Have you built close relationships with the young people in governance?
☐	☐	☐	Do you keep your commitment to young people consistent, not letting them be overshadowed by "more important" meetings and commitments?
☐	☐	☐	Do you make sure young people are given the opportunity to speak on every issue, not just program issues?
☐	☐	☐	If youth are confused about an issue, do you respond and give them the information they need?
☐	☐	☐	Is equal weight given to youth opinions?
			Youth behavior *(For youth members to complete if present)*
☐	☐	☐	Do you take leadership roles whenever possible?
☐	☐	☐	Do you ask to be on committees?
☐	☐	☐	Do you take initiative in getting to know all the members of your governing body on a personal level?
☐	☐	☐	Do you share your thoughts and ask questions, even when you are not comfortable doing so?
☐	☐	☐	Do you advocate for policies that promote young people's power (e.g., youth on committees, etc.)?
☐	☐	☐	Do you feel comfortable enough to constructively challenge/question patronizing behavior?
☐	☐	☐	Do you represent other young people's views?

Step 5: Training

Yes	N/A	To consider	
☐	☐	☐	Do you have an orientation system in place?
☐	☐	☐	Do you provide training for young people on speaking up in adult groups?
☐	☐	☐	Is there training for adults on understanding young people and being their allies?
☐	☐	☐	Do you offer training for young people and adults in general governance skills?

 14 Points © Youth on Board 1999   58 Day Street, P.O. Box 440322, Somerville, MA 02144 • 617.623.9900 x1242

POINT NUMBER 3

Determine Your Model for Youth Involvement

1 2 3 4 5 6 7 8 9 10 11 12 13 14

This chapter outlines possible ways to involve young people in your organization, school, or city. We discuss why choosing a model or structure is important, and then explore various options, using examples of different models to illustrate the points that should be considered.

I f you know you want to involve young people in a leadership role but aren't sure how, or if already have young people involved in the decision-making processes of your organization and are ready to try different approaches, this chapter can help you think about your options. Some of the suggestions that follow are better suited for groups that have overwhelming support for young people's involvement, while others are better for groups that want to start out slowly and increase their investment over time.

As you read this chapter, give some thought to the attitudes and beliefs of the other people in your organization. Are they really supportive, or just semi-committed to the idea of young people's involvement? Have you given people enough room to honestly discuss this issue among themselves? Allowing people to voice their concerns, hesitations, and skepticism can be an important part of this process. Hear them out, but don't be afraid to challenge them to try again, be courageous, and do something new.

Two General Approaches

All of the approaches to youth involvement, though they can be defined in many different ways, fall into two general categories. The first is to **involve young people directly in an existing adult body**. For example, adding several youth positions to an existing board, task force, policy committee, church council, city commission, foundation board, or tribal council. Your biggest decision with this route is to decide if the positions will be voting, non-voting, or observing. The second strategy is to **set up an adjunct body**

consisting of young people only. With this strategy, you need to pay close attention to how this group gives input to your primary governing body, and what staff support is available to keep the group functioning well.

Below, we compare the two approaches. As you read, keep a mental list of the pros and cons for each as they relate specifically to your group and situation. Remember that there is no one "right" approach. What works for one group or organization may not work in another setting. Your focus should be on determining where your needs and interests intersect with a particular model.

If you're trying to make a decision about whether to add young people to a current governing body or to develop a new adjunct body, here are a few key concerns to consider:

	PROS	CONS
Adding Young People to Adult Structures	Young members often re-energize a group of adults, bringing new ideas and fresh approaches to doing business.	Young people may feel intimidated in a group of predominately adult members, and therefore may not participate as freely as they should.
	Young people are able to make real decisions and see actual progress resulting from their work.	If you have a majority of board members under age 18, you may have to consider some legal issues (see *Point 6: Address Legal Issues*).
	Including young people in decisions made by your group compels adult members to buy into the theory that the opinions of young people are vital to the function of your organization.	Because youth representation usually only counts for a minority of total board membership, only a few young voices will be heard. This can lead to feelings of tokenism among young members.

	PROS	CONS
Creating an Adjunct Body Just for Young People	Young people have a less intimidating, less formal place to openly discuss issues and practice decision-making and meeting-participation skills.	If the adjunct body doesn't have a defined role that is fully acknowledged by the governing body, it can easily fall apart or become disillusioned with the organization.
	An adjunct body can serve as a training ground for new young members of a governing structure.	Adjunct groups often have limited authority because adults may struggle with sharing power with a group of young people. So, new members may receive limited real decision-making training.
	This type of structure allows input from a large number of young people.	It takes more staff time to maintain recruitment, training, and support of an active group.
	An adjunct body can take on more than one role—it can advise, evaluate, and run events and programs.	If too much time is spent on program issues, the adjunct body's advisory role can be lost. Be sure that all roles of the body are clearly defined.
	An adjunct body can provide valuable input to a specific project or issue.	The full board doesn't receive the full benefit that participation by young people brings.

Structural Options

What follows is a brief description of the most common structural options used by various organizations, followed by real-life examples. (All 501(c)(3) organizations have a board of directors as their primary governing body; these options are in addition to the board of directors.) Remember that all of these options can be considered decision-making bodies, but the responsibilities of each are different. Additionally, these options can include youth and adults, or just youth. As you read, keep in mind that there are many ways that you can more fully integrate young people into your organization, council, or board. A number of models have emerged over the past few years that have gained widespread acceptance, but don't let yourself be limited by them. Your options for how to involve young people are limited only by your imagination.

Advisory board

An advisory board offers regular feedback and advice to an organization, governing body, or individual. The group meets regularly and gives input on particular issues as requested by the governing body. The group can also take on other projects, such as events. In most cases, the advisory board has no governing authority or programmatic function. It is critical to define the advisory board's role and function before recruiting young people to be members. It is a mistake to set up an advisory board that is underutilized or not given sufficient authority to make recommendations.

Example:
Generations, Inc., a Boston-based nonprofit organization that brings youth and elders together, has a 10-member Kids Board that advises the Board of Directors on all program areas. The Kids Board also produces a newsletter about the different neighborhood projects in progress.

Policy committee

Policy committees, unlike many advisory boards, have an institutionalized role in the organization, according to the organization's bylaws. They serve in a significant advisory capacity in all areas, from programs and hiring to budget and organizational issues. However, they do not necessarily have representation on the board. It is possible that there would be a representative from a policy commit-tee sitting on the board generally or when the policy committee is advising the board in a specific area.

Example:
YouthBuild USA, based in Somerville, MA, and its affiliates have a policy committee that meet on a regular basis in order for corps members and alumni to give input and feedback. They discuss many of the same issues that the board is wrestling with, and their input is vital at the board level when decisions are being made. In certain areas, including hiring and firing, this committee serves as the decision-making body.

Program committee

Similar to an advisory board, a program committee offers support and feedback to the governing board, particularly around specific projects. They don't have any governing authority, although their input is important to a governing body. The main difference is the length and scope of responsibilities: program committees are usual-ly convened around a specific program or project, whereas advisory committees can advise on all aspects of an organization's operations.

Example:
Knoxville's (TN) Promise–Alliance for Youth formed a youth council to help with the planning of their Regional Youth Summit. The youth council was responsible for setting goals for the youth and adult tracks at the summit, planning a service project for the event, and facilitating roundtable discussions on the day of the event.

Grant-making committee

This committee consists of a group of people that make decisions on how to allocate funds to community projects. Among the duties performed by grant-making committees are to set funding guidelines, reviews grants, make site visits, and raise funds.

Example:
The Ewing Marion Kauffman Foundation's Youth Development Division created a board that brings together teens from the greater Kansas City area to exchange ideas about the needs of young people. The Youth Advisory Board sets policy and guides the distribution of special grants from the Kauffman Foundation. They create requests for proposals, meet to review applicants, conduct site visits, and give grants of up to $5,000 for youth-led projects for youth service and youth leadership in the urban core of Kansas City.

Commission

Commissions are fully autonomous entities. Rather than acting as an adjunct to an organization or city office, they are usually set up to advance policies and recommendations for a community or organization.

Example:
San Francisco has a number of commissions that advise the city in areas ranging from human services to city planning. Many of these groups are advised by young people who provide input and advise on policy. In particular, the San Francisco Youth Commission assists other city departments and commissions to include youth voices and perspectives.

Task force

A task force is usually a short-term entity that is created for a specific purpose.

Example:
The Ford Foundation, based in New York City, established the Youth Commission on Urban Poverty several summers ago to bring together six young people from around the country to spend the summer studying urban poverty and producing a report for the Foundation's board. Although they called it a commission, we would classify it as a task force because it had a short life and a specific focus.

Our Recommendations

At Youth on Board, we have been studying the many options of youth governance structures since our founding in 1994. As such, there are options that we believe work best, based on all we have observed.

Combine options

First, we recommend that you add at least two youth board members with voting privileges to your governing structure or to your council, board, church vestry, etc. Also, create a youth advisory board that feeds into and off of the youth board members, as well as being responsible for other projects. We find that this model works best because both youth board members and the youth advisory board have a clear set of responsibilities and a concrete reporting structure. This model is used by the board of the Georgia Campaign for Adolescent Pregnancy Prevention. This board, chaired by founder Jane Fonda, created a Youth Leadership Council for advisory purposes, and two young people from the Youth Leadership Council serve, with voting privileges, on the main board.

Youth policy committee

If your adult governing structure is hesitant to add young members and you decide to create an adjunct body, we recommend creating a youth policy committee. Ideally, this board should report to the governing body through more than one youth representative who sits on the board when necessary, as outlined above.

The mistakes

The most common mistake occurs when young people are on adjunct bodies where there is a lack of clarity about exactly what the young people's responsibilities are.

Just as we have been able to observe which structures work best, Youth on Board has also witnessed a number of failures. We find that the most common mistake occurs when young people are on adjunct bodies where there is a lack of clarity about exactly what the young people's responsibilities are. Also, we find that, because of a lack of education on the topic of youth governance, adults may have exceedingly high, or equally low, expectations of what young people are to accomplish. Lastly, young people are often not told about the limit of their power and authority, no matter the capacity in which they serve.

A Few Words on Implementation

Regardless of the specific structure you choose, there are a few key steps that will make the process go more smoothly. Here are a few tips to keep in mind as you make your final decision.

If you are considering adding young people to a current governing body:

◆ Add two or three young people at the same time. Anything less can too easily amount to token representation that will fail.

◆ Be ready to implement a thorough training program for both young people and adults.

If you are considering setting up a new, adjunct body:

◆ Be clear about this group's role and scope of power. Make sure that the governing body agrees upon the role of this group and is willing to share authority in particular areas where the body will be advisors or decision makers.

◆ Make sure that you have staff or board members assigned and ready to devote time and energy to getting the group recruited, oriented, and ready to do their job.

◆ Make sure that there is a link between your governing body and this group—someone who conveys important information between the two groups. You don't want two groups moving forward separately.

In any case, we recommend that you read this book thoroughly and carefully, because all the information you need is right here.

How Do You Choose?

Figuring out how to choose an approach to involving youth in your organization is no simple task. You want to think carefully about what you need, and what you are able to support. Some options require time, while others need flexibility. Use the questionnaire below to help you determine the profile of a structure that will work best for your organization. Your answers to the following "yes" or "no" questions can help you better determine whether you should add young people to an existing structure, or create an adjunct body just for youth.

Adding Young People to an Existing Structure

Yes   No

☐   ☐   Are the adults in my organization committed to the idea of involving youth in decision making? If not, can I convince them it's a good idea?

☐   ☐   Are the members of my current structure willing to make things youth-friendly?

☐   ☐   Does the law in my state allow people below the age of 18 to be voting members of a board of directors?

☐   ☐   Is my organization willing to change its bylaws to reflect a requirement of young members on our governing structure?

☐   ☐   Is my organization willing to add more than one young person?

Creating an Adjunct Group for Young People

☐   ☐   Does my organization have the time and resources to start something new?

☐   ☐   Do I have to get agreement from my colleagues and/or my boss?

☐   ☐   Does my organization have access to, or can we gain access to, enough young people to create a separate group?

☐   ☐   Do we have the budget to support an adjunct group?

☐   ☐   Do we have a clear set of responsibilities for an adjunct group?

POINT NUMBER 4

Identify Organizational Barriers

This chapter outlines common organizational barriers to involving young people in governance structures, and suggests systems you can establish to ensure success.

As much as we would like the practice of youth in governance programs to work without a hitch, things usually don't happen that way. There are often limiting attitudes and logistical challenges that can prevent young people from functioning well on a governing body or program committee. One of the reasons many adults do not involve young people in meaningful governance positions is that it can be a lot of work. By committing to youth governance, you are taking on the challenge of changing attitudes, structures, and behaviors, and this is never easy. Look forward to and grow from the challenges. All positive change takes hard work and is very satisfying in the end.

As you read this chapter, think about barriers you have faced with other efforts within your group. For example, was there a time when you tried to reach out to a different constituency? What challenges did you face in recruiting and maintaining that group's involvement? Is there a time when you worked to change your group's attitude about a situation? Was it necessary for you to bring up the idea quietly and have it grow on people over a period of several months? Or did you throw out an idea and ask that people respond to it immediately? Think about the way your group works best. What barriers are likely to pop up for you and your governing body as you work to involve young people in a more meaningful way?

While you should expect some challenges, you should avoid reinventing the wheel. Here we offer lessons other organizations have learned when facing their own barriers, and we lead you through processes for identifying potential pitfalls and developing strong solutions.

By committing to youth governance, you are taking on the challenge of changing attitudes, structures, and behaviors, and this is never easy.

Identify Organizational Barriers

There are four major organizational barriers that will throw a wrench into any youth leadership program: bylaws that have not been changed, conflict of interest issues, legality questions, and no dedicated budget.

Bylaws

By institutionalizing youth involvement in the form of changing your bylaws, your organization accomplishes several things:
(1) It sends a strong message that the members of your governing structure buy into the youth in governance idea; (2) It ensures that young people will be vital members of your governance group long after the present staff or current members leave; and (3) It legally shows commitment to giving young people a place on your board and sends the message to young people that they deserve a place in the decision-making process of your organization. At its best, youth governance is an institutional commitment, not a project of one or even a few individuals.

A general note for any organization is to be specific about the age of youth on your governing body. Be sure to distinguish between young people and young adults. This eliminates the possibility that a 27-year-old, for example, might pass for the "young person" in your organization's governing body. It also helps to specify the number of years young people should serve. We recommend that only a maximum age be specified (e.g., that young people no more than 20 years old may serve). Who's to say a 12-year-old can't serve?

Sample bylaws

Are you wondering what changes can be made to your group's bylaws in order to include youth leaders on a permanent basis? Here are some sample bylaws you may want to consider:

• Below are two sections taken from the bylaws of S.C.A.L.E. (Student Coalition for Action in Literacy Education), an organization that pairs college students with people learning to read. They clearly state how many youth must be on the board, and the length of their terms.

Section 1. The Board shall consist of 13 to 18 members elected by the Board between the Spring and Summer meetings for staggered, three-year terms. College and university students shall be elected to either a two or three year term.

Section 2. Board members will come from the following areas: college faculty and administration, new readers, college students, foundations, corporations, unions, media, national service organizations, literacy practitioners, and others interested in the [organization's] mission. A minimum of four college and university students and two new readers shall serve on the Board.

• The following example is from a Girl Scout Council.

Article 1—The Council

2. <u>Voting Membership</u>. The voting members of the council shall consist of:

A. delegates elected by area associations;

B. members of the board of directors;

C. members of the council nominating committee;

D. National Council delegates not otherwise members of the council.

<u>Eligibility</u>. All voting members of the council shall be adult volunteers and girls 14 years of age and over who are members of the Girl Scout movement registered through the council.

- This last example is taken from the bylaws of YouthBuild:

> **Section 3.** Ex-Officio Directors. The board of directors shall include one (1) representative of the YouthBuild Philadelphia Policy Committee as an ex-officio, voting member of the board, and such additional ex-officio, voting members as the board may from time to time determine. After their year of ex-officio service the youth members may be nominated at the board's discretion to regular board membership through the nominating process.

Conflict of interest

Organizational leaders are sometimes concerned that involving a young program participant in governance will create a conflict of interest. This can be easily addressed by establishing a simple but clearly written conflict of interest policy. Conflict of interest policies are often no more than a single succinct paragraph that clearly outlines the group's policy. When drafting or amending your own conflict of interest policy, always consult an attorney, since legal guidelines do vary from state to state. Consider the following form taken from the National Center for Nonprofit Boards' publication, *How to Manage Conflict of Interest: A Guide for Nonprofit Boards*:

> In the case that a board or committee member is aware of a potential conflict of interest with respect to any matter coming before the board or committee, she or he will not be present for voting in connection with the matter. She or he may, however, participate fully in discussion of the matter prior to the vote.
>
> **Signature:** _____
>
> **Date:** _____

Questions of legality

You might be wondering, "Is it even legal for young people to sit on a board of directors?" Admittedly, the issue of legality can be a concern. In 43 states, the law is "silent" on the issue of young people serving on boards of directors, meaning there is no specific law that addresses the issue. This lack of legal clarity understandably makes some people nervous. However, many organizations have overcome these concerns simply by becoming familiar with their state's laws, consulting an attorney with experience in this area, and drafting conflict of interest forms. All three steps are covered in much greater detail in *Point 6: Address Legal Issues*.

No dedicated budget

Adding young people to your governance structure or decision-making process takes more than time and dedication. There are costs involved that are often overlooked until the needs arise. Transportation to and from meetings for young people is an expense that your organization should cover. Staff time will be needed to support young people (calling them before meetings, keeping in touch with them and their parents between meetings, etc.). Additionally, because they may take place right after school, your organization will want to provide food at meetings, whereas food was never provided before. Other expenses will arise that will make you wish your organization had a dedicated budget line item for board activities.

Other Barriers

What other barriers might get in the way of your efforts to involve youth in governance? To answer this question, consider common barriers in your organization that prevent good ideas from being implemented, and address them at the outset. For example, if the biggest barrier for your organization is money, keep this in mind from the beginning. When you start dreaming about a youth retreat or training for your board, make everyone aware that you need to do this initiative with no budget. Or, approach this barrier from a different direction. There are avenues for funding in the area of youth in governance; do a little research to see what's available.

By planning for ways to address barriers in the beginning, you won't be caught off guard when they occur. Also, other board members and staff will likely be more supportive when they see that you have thought through the ramifications of this initiative.

Consider the following questions as you think about likely barriers within your organization or governance structure:

- What barriers does this group regularly run into (e.g., attendance)?

- When several members disagree about something, what has traditionally inhibited the conversation or made it difficult to move forward?

- What strategies have been effective in moving the group forward?

- What support does the group need in order to face potential barriers with greater courage, grace, and persistence?

Following are more pitfalls that can get in the way of successfully involving young people in governance and community efforts:

Poor recruitment strategies

Poor recruitment can be another hazard to successful youth decision making. Organizations too often reach for the easiest, quickest solution to youth involvement and consequently choose someone who might not be right for the job. The young person might be over-committed in other areas, inexperienced, or not really interested in the position. Putting in the time up front to develop a thorough recruitment plan and then recruiting strong participants is critical to long-term success. *Point 7: Recruit Young People* covers this issue at great length.

We recommend drafting a letter of agreement that details your expectations for new board members.

Unclear or low expectations

Occasionally, young people encounter problems on boards because they have signed up for something they don't understand. There are a wide range of activities and rules concerning board work that adults take for granted, but that young people may not know or understand. For example, your committee may assume that each member will contribute to the annual fundraising campaign. This is something you might not mention to new, young members, but when the annual campaign rolls around, the assumption still stands. Things can get awkward for young people or adults because expectations weren't clear, and young people may not feel comfortable meeting them.

It is likely that young people won't know the right questions to ask when they join a board, especially if they've never been on one before. In addition to conducting a thorough orientation process, we recommend drafting a letter of agreement that details your expectations for new board members, and sharing it with young people when they are selected for your youth governance position. As you design the orientation, put yourself in their shoes and try to imagine the questions they might have—both the obvious and obscure aspects of the job. Refer to *Point 8: Create a Strong Orientation Process* for further details.

Lack of support

Remember that adult work settings are a new environment for many young people. They may not recognize when they need help or be able to articulate the problems they are encountering. Think of their situation like a visit to a foreign land. You don't understand the traffic rules or cultural etiquette, so you walk around on pins and needles fearing that you are making a mistake or about to make one. You're so lost you don't even know how to ask for help. This is how many young people feel in this new environment. They may feel misunderstood, unrecognized, and ill-prepared, even when they are fully capable of making significant contributions.

Ways that adults can support young people are covered in greater detail in *Point 13: Build Youth/Adult Relationships*. Some general tips include: talk with youth individually about their concerns or questions; give them extra information through articles or success stories; assign mentors; assist with transportation; and have staff assist youth in understanding how they can be most effective in this new environment.

Language

Young people and adults often speak different languages—quite literally. While young people might use words or hand gestures that adults don't understand or are uncomfortable with, adults might use phrases and body language that young people find intimidating or frustrating. In a committee meeting, it is not uncommon to hear words and abbreviations such as RFP, "in the red," "in the black," and 501(c)(3) status. These are just a few of the terms that young people may not know.

Consider keeping an ongoing list of tag words during meetings. Adults and young people can tag a word during a meeting by raising their hand. The word gets defined and added to a list that is reviewed at the beginning of each meeting. You can make this a fun ice-breaking exercise to remind people that there is a mix of cultures and languages in the room. People should be encouraged to list words so everyone feels like there is room at the table for not knowing a word or gesture. Remember, it will take time, effort, and patience to develop a shared understanding.

Another activity you can do with your group is the Jargon Game. Have young people and adults divide into separate groups and brainstorm all of the potential jargon they can imagine someone using in a given meeting. Then write the words on index cards. Pull a card from the stack, and have board members guess the meaning

Talk with youth individually about their concerns or questions.

of each word. You can also divide the group into teams and keep score of words that each team defines accurately.

Stereotypes

Another roadblock to effective board relationships is the stereotypes that adults and youth carry about each other. Neither group may have given much thought about or addressed the negative assumptions they hold about the other. Yet, stereotypes are reinforced everywhere in our culture, and they obstruct productive partnerships between generations. Everyone in the group needs to work on identifying and eliminating their stereotypes. If you discuss and address them openly, your group will be better able to move past them and work effectively together.

4

STORIES FROM THE STREET

What often happens between young people and adults is that one thing is said, another understood. Consider this scenario from the community development organization XCEL, Inc.[1]:

"That's the bomb," Sophia, age 16, said about a new program initiative presented at a recent board meeting. In response, John, the board chair, remarked, "Well then, what are we doing wrong? How does this initiative need to be changed?" Sophia looked back at him in confusion. What was he talking about?

Not sure where he was coming from, she mumbled, "I'm not sure," then fell silent. The meeting continued. Adults listed 10 ways in which the initiative could look different. At the end of the meeting Sophia, now completely frustrated, said, "I don't know why you guys are doing this. I said it was the bomb. Didn't what I say mean anything?" At last, another board member stopped and tentatively asked, "Bomb means 'good?'" "Of course!" Sophia said.

[1] XCEL Inc., 16 Brookfield Street, Norwalk, CT 06851. Phone: 203/845-9556.

Potential Roadblocks

Gather members of your committee, task force, board, or council, complete with young people and adults, and divide them into small groups. Have each group draw up recommendations for how to address each of the potential roadblocks listed below. After small group work, you may want to have a large group discussion about the various recommendations. Remember that there are no stock solutions to these and other potential roadblocks. Be creative in your approaches to solving problems.

Potential Roadblock	Recommendations
Adults dominate discussions of committees and regular meetings, despite concerns about this problem raised by young board members.	
You feel your governance structure could benefit from a youth/adult retreat, but budget constraints do not allow for one.	
Young people need supervision and guidance in order to be effective, yet adult board members and staff have no time to devote to them.	

Potential Roadblock   ## Recommendations

Your board has decided it
wants to include young
members, yet nobody on the
board knows any young people
to invite as participants.

Young people need
transportation to and from
meetings, and complain of
missing dinner to attend
meetings, yet there is no
money to cover travel or
food expenses.

Your council had two young
members last year, but both of
them have left to go to college.
You now have a new council
president who doesn't know
youth were involved, and
nobody seems to be telling her.

Other potential roadblocks:

5

Overcome Attitudinal Barriers

This chapter outlines major attitudinal barriers that prevent effective youth/adult partnerships and suggests strategies for eliminating them.

Adults who work with young people (parents, counselors, advocates, etc.) care deeply about them and work hard to make the world a better place for them.[1] Unfortunately, that doesn't prevent these adults from unconsciously holding beliefs that keep young people from being all that they can be. We've all been young, and deep down we know we've all felt disrespected at one time or another. But when we grow into adulthood, we tend to forget what it was like to be young and often fall into the same patterns of adult behavior that we despised as youth.

Adults often have misconceptions about young people because we've been taught throughout our lives that they are somehow inferior. When, in fact, young people are powerful, bursting with energy and intelligence. Young people are fully human—they already are complete and capable individuals. Yet, our present society often treats them as if they are "in training" to become human beings. Those under the age of 21 are often not respected solely because of their age. The excuse for treating young people this way is an assumed, or actual, lack of experience, knowledge, and intelligence.

This is not about placing blame. It's about supporting young people, building relationships with them, realizing ways that they are being disrespected, and working with them to improve our organizations and society as a whole. To do that, we need to understand the hidden barriers that prevent youth/adult partnerships from working as effectively as they might.

---

[1] The majority of the text in this chapter was taken from the Resource Center for Youth and their Allies pamphlet *Get the Word Out!* and the pamphlet *Understanding and Supporting Young People* by Jenny Sazama.

The Role of Power Dynamics

The way our society is structured, older people have more power than younger people do. In general, adults have access to more resources and information than young people. In contrast, young people have fewer resources and rights. This creates a power dynamic we call "adultism." Adultism is a term applied to any behavior, action, language, or limitation placed on young people's rights that does not afford them the respect that they deserve as human beings. It is often predicated on the belief that, because someone is young, they lack intelligence or ability.

Young people grow up fighting to be heard, trying to change the opinions of adults in their lives, and trying not to internalize feelings of unimportance.

Having a hard time imagining that young people are treated as "less than" adults? Think of it this way: How many adults do you know who cast off responsibility, make unwise decisions despite knowing better, or are well-informed about intoxication yet still hop in a car after a night of partying and drive home drunk? Why do we characterize these adults as acting "childishly?" There are many young people who balance doing well in school with holding down a part-time job and playing sports; who practically raise their siblings and themselves when adults in their lives leave them or let them down; and, as may be the case in your own organization, who take on leadership roles and make decisions that have an impact on their peers and their communities. Yet, these young people are not given credit for their behavior. Young people grow up fighting to be heard, trying to change the opinions of adults in their lives, and trying not to internalize feelings of unimportance.

Adultism and Society

Do you remember a day, back when you were 8 or 9, when someone told you, "You can't do that?you're not old enough"? Unfortunately, this message is reinforced throughout our childhood. Young people are kept from experiences and information because adults think they are not ready. Sometimes they aren't, and sometimes they are; the point is that they are seldom given a chance.

We grow up believing what we are told about ourselves and other young people. Young people internalize messages that tell them they are less capable, less insightful, and less valuable than adults are. As a result, they often feel like they don't have anything important to say or that they have to wait until they are older to act on their ideas.

As they internalize these negative messages, young people begin to treat one another with disrespect. They attack each other for being different in any way—for getting good grades or for wearing shoes that aren't in style. They act out adultism within their own peer groups. After years of hearing that kids are lazy, kids are delinquents, kids are slackers, and kids should be seen and not heard, young people start to believe these stereotypes. They forget their own value and the value of their peers.

Worse yet, this thinking is passed on through the generations, continually alienating a talented and valuable segment of our society. Consider these facts:

- At the age of 12, Craig Kielburger founded Free the Children, an international network of children helping children to end child labor. He is now 15 and lives in Toronto.[2]

- Joan of Arc led 3,000 French knights to victory in the Battle of Orleans when she was 17.

- Danny Seo, now 20, founded Earth 2000—a national organization of young people who are concerned about animal rights and the environment—when he was 12.[3]

[2] Taken from information posted on the Website www.freethechildren.org.
[3] Taken from information posted on the Website www.amazon.com.

- Mozart composed his first symphony at age 6.

- W.E.B. DuBois was published in his hometown newspaper by the age of 14.

- Einstein wrote his first paper on the theory of relativity when he was 16.

Why do we find these facts surprising? Do we truly expect so much less from young people? Instead of expecting excellence and initiative from young people, are we too focused on trying to coddle or control them? What great discoveries and advancements are we as a society sacrificing by not encouraging and helping young people to take the lead? Perhaps young people should be in the lead.

The effect on adults

Adults are not left unscathed by adultism, which has repercussive effects on the adult population. When we become adults, we don't really forget the effect that adultism had on us as young people. That adultism affected us is evident in some of the ways we treat each other and the ways we value, or undervalue, certain professions. Consider these examples:

- Caring for children is seen as "women's work," and as such is undervalued.

- Teachers, nannies, babysitters, and child-care workers are usually paid comparatively low wages.

- Parents are scapegoats for almost any problem that occurs with young people. They are publicly blamed for not "properly" taking care of, or raising, their children.

It is no one's fault that adultism occurs in our society, but we can all do something to stop it. Just by reading this book, you are challenging the belief that young people can't take on responsible leadership positions. The adults on your governing body need to be conscious of how they use the power they have as members, and of

That adultism affects us is evident in some of the ways we treat each other and the ways we value, or undervalue, certain professions.

how they can share it with young people. Encourage your board members to read this chapter, complete the worksheets at the end, and discuss how they see power dynamics operating within your group. Are they holding back opportunities for young people to participate and lead? Where do young people need encouragement to see themselves as responsible and talented enough to take the lead?

Tips for Changing Attitudes

Here are some tips to help you work on shifting attitudes about young people and adults:

Appreciate people

Sincerely appreciate and notice the ways that adults are good allies to young people. ("I noticed the way you listened to LaTanya and backed her up when people were being unfair to her.") Also notice and appreciate the ways that young people back each other up. ("It was great that you would not let Greg bad-mouth Maria in front of her friends. I'm glad you stuck by her.") Avoid cutting people down. Instead, point out the things they do well. With a bit of forethought, you can find things you appreciate about people even if you don't know them well. Appreciating people is one of the best ways to demonstrate that you really care, even if you and that person don't always agree. Appreciation can never be overdone if it's sincere.

Take pride in being an adult

It's true that until you love yourself, you cannot truly love others. As adults, we need to be in touch with our joy in, and curiosity for, life and adventure. Young people need to see adults leading full, satisfying lives—lives with no limits. Too often, young people characterize adulthood as a boring and miserable existence. And as adults, too many of us give youth no reason to think otherwise. We have the chance to contradict the image of adults that youth have. Working with young people can help us remember that life should be fun.

Pay attention to language

Instead of defining young people only by their age and referring to them as "children," "kids," or "students," try calling them simply "people" or "friends." Language is an extremely effective way to raise awareness. When we begin to think of and talk about young people as just people, instead of defining them by age, we work to break down age-related stereotypes.

Adultism vs. Ageism

You may be wondering why we use the term "adultism" to describe an age-related attitude and behavior pattern. The truth is, the term "ageism" was already taken. Ageism is discrimination based on age, especially against middle-aged and elderly people, as defined by The American Heritage Dictionary. Adultism differs from ageism in that adultism is targeted at young people.

Understand the struggle of being a parent

Parents have the most direct influence on young people's lives. Raising a child is no small undertaking. A huge segment of the parent population is overworked, under-supported, and criticized. Parents deserve tons of patience and support. When working with young people, it is important to establish a personal relationship with their parents. Get to know them. Respect them! Share with them your ideas about empowering young people. Remember that they are as concerned as you are about young people and can make wonderful allies.

Help young people talk about adultism

Adult allies need to speak on behalf of young people, but this is never a substitute for, or as effective as, young people speaking for themselves about issues that affect them. As adult allies, we can set up situations where youth can talk about their lives in adult settings. We can also encourage them to talk to their friends.

Check competitiveness at the door

Most of us would admit to having a competitive streak. But, the world of adult allies is no place for contests. It does not make sense to compete with other adults over who is the "best" ally to young people—who can do more for whom and how. This kind of attitude will prevent you from supporting others and building a network of adult allies. We all have to work together in order for real and lasting accomplishments to be made.

Be sensitive to dissenting opinions

Before you broach the subject of power dynamics between young people and adults, remember that there are adults who will not agree with you. There are no "good guys" or "bad guys" here. Those who are uncomfortable with young people having power are not inherently bad, and those of us acting on behalf of young people aren't inherently saintly.

When someone openly disagrees with you, you may become frustrated and be tempted to stop talking with that person. Instead, try calming yourself down and sincerely listening to what he or she is saying. Exchange ideas, and remember that in every disagreement there is common ground. Find it. The goal should be to build allies, not to alienate people. This may mean respecting ideological differences as much as racial, age, or religious differences. We don't have to agree on every detail to care equally about the success of young people.

The Role of Adult Allies

Adults play a critical role as allies to young people. Because they have more power in society than young people, adults can open doors and create opportunities for them. Youth need adults to be real with them, not rule over them. They need adults to respect them, just as young people are expected to be respectful to adults.

What is an adult ally? Someone who:

- speaks on behalf of young people and their rights, and makes room for young people to speak for themselves whenever possible;

- helps young people communicate effectively in adult settings so that they are treated fairly and equally;

- reminds young people that their ideas are important and that they have a lot to say;

- understands that it makes complete sense for us to make friends with many people, including people of many different age groups;

- wants to show young people how to overcome the artificial separations (such as those based on race, sex, age, etc.) that tend to divide us from one another;

- is open to learning from young people;

- works to model for young people a different picture of adulthood—where adults enjoy friendships with other adults, live fun and exciting lives, and don't just work all the time—than the one of rigidity usually offered by society; and

- helps young people support each other and take themselves seriously.

The role of adult allies is discussed further in *Point 13: Build Youth/Adult Relationships* and *Point 14: Create Support Networks*.

Consider this example of adultism in action. Young people in Vernon, CT, are waging a fight against a teen curfew law in their town. Listen to how International Student Activism Alliance[4] Representative Stratos Pahis describes the struggle in the February 1999 issue of The Students' Voice: "As teen curfews are being more widely used across the United States, our rights as students and as Americans are being violated. After all, this is the USA, the land of the free, where justice is for all. How can a government tell a certain population of innocent citizens that they mustn't leave their homes during certain hours? How can a group of people be placed on house arrest even if they have done nothing wrong?

"...After four years of being confined to their homes after 11 p.m. on weekdays and midnight on weekends, the teens of Vernon decided that they had had enough. ...We had to do something of our own to help get rid of this ridiculous law. ...We decided that the first logical step would be to circulate a petition in school and present it to the town council. ... After the presentation of over 700 signatures, the council took a vote ... and even though the council voted to keep the curfew for another year, three members abstained, marking the first time any council members abstained on the annual curfew vote since its inception. ...But it wasn't enough.

"...The curfew hasn't been repealed yet, but as a result of the actions taken by us, the council decided to amend the curfew law. Now minors can be outside during curfew hours as long as they are exercising their First Amendment rights while doing so. Yeah, it's a stupid exception, and yeah, it makes the curfew virtually unenforceable. ...But it's at least an improvement that we, the students, people who can't vote or hold public office, directly created.

"If there is a curfew in your town or city, don't just sit there. Get up and do something about it! Curfews don't work and they are plain discriminatory. ...And anyway, if they work as good as the police like to think they do, why not have one for adults also? The fact of the matter is that curfews violate our rights, and if we don't stick up for ourselves, who will?"

[4] International Student Activism Alliance, 31 North Quaker Lane, West Hartford, CT 06119. Website: www.studentactivism.org.

WORKSHEET

Adultism 101

The following exercises can help put you on the path to changing attitudes about young people and adults. They are best conducted with a mixed group of young people and adults.

Exercise 1: Negative Messages Brainstorm

How does adultism play out in society? Have your group brainstorm negative messages about young people that they have heard or hear now. Consider these examples that may seem familiar to you as you look back on your childhood:

Young people are told:

• "You don't need to know that. Wait until you are older."

• "Don't worry, you wouldn't understand this anyway."

• "Children should be seen and not heard."

• "When you are older, you might be able to do this."

• "Do as I say, not as I do."

• "Act your age."

• "It's just a stage, you'll grow out of it."

Young people are:

• forgotten when communities sit down to do problem solving;

• left out of conversations concerning their education and educational systems;

• "protected" from many real-life situations and problems that they may be capable of handling.

Explain that at some point in our lives, we've all experienced unfair treatment because of our age. It is important for everyone to remember the negative ways youth are sometimes treated. This exercise should involve lighthearted discussion.

 58 Day Street, P.O. Box 440322, Somerville, MA 02144 • 617.623.9900 x1242

Exercise 2: Adultist Role Play: The Broken Heart's Club

This role-playing skit illustrates one aspect of adultist behavior. Assemble a cast of characters from volunteers in your group and have them act out this scene. After the "play," discuss reactions.

The scenario: Shawna comes home after a rotten day at school. She and Todd have been going out for five months now and he just called it off. Bill, her dad, notices that Shawna looks down, but when he finds out the problem he completely dismisses Shawna's hurt over this break-up. He acts as if because she's young her feelings aren't real.

Cast of Characters:

Shawna Bloodworth—heartbroken young person.
After five months you've really grown to care about Todd. Not only is he your boyfriend, he is your best friend, and it's really sad to imagine life without him. Your dad notices something is wrong and he completely blows you off when he hears about your breakup with Todd.

Shawna might say, "Sheesh Dad, why do you think it's just puppy love? Just because I don't have my driver's license doesn't mean that I don't have real feelings."

Bill Bloodworth—Shawna's oblivious dad.
It seems just crazy to you how kids think they have the weight of the world on their shoulders. What you would give to have their little worries.

Bill might say, "Oh buck up now. You still haven't gone through a real break-up. The alimony I'm paying your mother—Now *that's* something to cry about!"

Terri Sweet—Shawna's dad's girlfriend.
You've noticed that whenever Shawna is around Todd, her boyfriend, she just swoons. She seems just crazy about him. You don't want to get in the middle of anything, but her dad Bill is being awfully insensitive.

Terri might say, "Shawna, I didn't want to say anything in front of your father because there seemed to be some tension, but here's my phone number—just in case you want to talk about things."

Need an extra character? Add a scene at the beginning during which Shawna and Todd break up.

Exercise 3: Develop an Image of a World Without Adultism

By imagining a world without adultism, people often come to understand how adultism inhibits young people every day. Use the following scenarios to stimulate discussion about the legal and cultural barriers to young people's power.

Imagine if...

... young people in every school were supported and trained to participate in hiring their teachers, and had a say in the way their schools were run. Why doesn't this currently happen? How might it work?

... politicians were as accountable to young people in their districts as they are to the adults. What changes would be made?

... young people had the money to buy high-priced items, including cars and houses. Would they be treated with more respect and given more attention in stores and malls?

Help others define adultism

By crafting a formal definition of their own, people come to understand adultism more deeply. As we've learned in community development and in education, people feel ownership for buildings, concepts, and even definitions that they have a hand in creating.

Exercise 4 (for Youth): Help Young People Understand Their Inner Struggles

This exercise helps young people recognize the negative feelings they harbor about their peers and also help them feel proud about themselves. Give each young person in the group a piece of paper and a pen. Ask the following questions, one by one, and have each person record brief answers for one minute. Then, ask people in the group to volunteer answers to each question. Note and discuss any similarities. The questions are:

• What can't you stand about other young people?

• Have you ever been in a fight, verbal or physical, with someone your age? What was it about?

• Do you think you are smart, and do you feel comfortable expressing your opinions? If so, why? If not, why not?

• What do you like about other young people?

Teen Years

The following exercise works best with small groups in which each person answers the following questions aloud. People should select one, two, or three questions to answer (depending on how much time you have). Then have each person share his or her answers. After a person's responses, there can be brief discussion, but only about that person's answers. This process ensures that everyone has a chance to speak uninterrupted.

As you're leading the Teen Years activity, throw in experiences from your own teen years—stories that demonstrate the humor and difficulty of being a teen will help your group to remember their own experiences. When working with teenagers, it is important for us to remember what it was like to be a teenager. Not only does this worksheet, adapted from the Oakland Men's Project, work well with all-adult groups, it's a great way to have teens and adults compare their lives.

Teen Years

If you are an adult, think back to your teen years and answer several of the following questions. If you are a teen, think about what your life is like right now and answer several of the following questions. If answering any of these questions out loud makes you uncomfortable, simply answer them on this sheet.

- My best friend was/is:

- The meanest thing a friend ever did to me was:

- What's a secret that you never told anyone?

- What was the most disgusting habit you had?

- What is the most powerful moment you remember having?

- My worst teacher was/is:

- An adult I trust(ed) was/is:

- My favorite game was/is:

- One thing I will never forget about my teen years is:

- What was your most embarrassing moment?

- Who is the adult who you trust(ed) most or who most understood you? What was s/he like? Did s/he know how much s/he made a difference in your life?

- What is/was your mother's main complaint about you? Your father's? As an adult, do you ever recognize that in your life now?

- The thing I most want(ed) to change about myself was/is:

- Another story from my teen years that I would like to share is:

- As an adult, one of the things I had forgotten about those years is:

To end this exercise, have the group discuss the following questions:

- What are your earliest memories of noticing that young people were not given the same respect as adults?

- Tell about a time that you did not give young people your full respect. It can be a subtle way, like being "too busy" to listen to what they had to say, or something as obvious telling someone to sit down and shut up because you said so.

- Talk about a time when you were an ally to young people and showed them that they had your full respect.

POINT
NUMBER

6

Address
Legal
Issues

*This chapter outlines legal
issues relating to youth
governance, and suggests
proactive measures you can
take against any potential
liability.*

*I*t is exciting to think about appointing young people to a board of directors.[1] They can offer an often underrepresented perspective on board issues. With their involvement, however, may come concern about the legal ramifications of having a minor vote on a governing body. Many organizations stay away from putting young people on boards for this very reason. Others simply feel like they don't know enough to move forward with youth representation on their board.

Your governing body may be asking questions such as, "Can people under 18 legally serve on our board? Will a young person's vote be considered legitimate? Will our board still be able to enter into formal contracts with a young person as a decision maker?" These are questions that are currently being raised all over the country. Although rulings about youth involvement vary from state to state, in general, young people are considered by law to be legitimate decision makers.

As you read through this chapter, think about resources you may have to help you further investigate legal issues in your state—pro bono lawyers, student interns, etc. Though most lawyers are supportive of this process, some are more helpful than others. Shop around, get several opinions, and remember that in most states legal issues are not insurmountable barriers. With planning and research, adding youth to your board can be legal and revolutionary action!

---

[1] Please note that in this chapter we are talking about boards of directors, specifically whether or not young people can legally *vote* on such boards. Young people can *serve* on any governance structure. However, it is important to note the distinction between voting and serving. If voting is considered a duty of serving on a particular board, and the law specifies a minimum age for board members, then young people below that age cannot serve in this capacity. When reading this chapter and interpreting the law in your particular state, watch for this distinction.

Five Frequently Asked Questions About the Legalities of Youth in Governance

We will address five frequently asked questions that arise when organizations, committees, and government offices look into the possibility of having young people serve on boards of directors:

1. What are the legal obligations of all board members, regardless of age?

2. Can young people legally serve on a board in my state?

3. When there is no law, what does it mean?

4. How is voting handled with young members on a board?

5. If the law in my state does not permit young people to vote on boards, how can I work to change the law or work around it?

Use this process to broaden your own knowledge of the legal system, and to educate the other board members and young people involved. People are often intimidated by the jargon and complexity of our legal system. Help them understand the legalities around youth governance.

As you move through this chapter, we encourage you to keep a list of your own questions. On the worksheet at the end of this chapter, there is a list of defined legal terms. Use the additional space on the worksheet to add other words and questions that emerge for you and other board members.

People are often intimidated by the jargon and complexity of our legal system. Help them understand the legalities around youth governance.

1. What are the legal obligations of all board members, regardless of age?

Before we discuss the legal issues surrounding the incorporation of youth onto boards, we offer a brief overview of what is expected of a nonprofit board of directors. These issues are critical to understanding the legal arguments both for and against allowing youth to serve on boards.

The obligations of board members [2]

Above all, the directors of a nonprofit corporation are bound by two general types of legal duties: a **duty of care**—the duty to perform their responsibilities in good faith and in a manner that they reasonably believe to be in the best interests of the corporation, and with such care as an ordinarily prudent person in a like position with respect to a similar corporation would use in similar circumstances; and a **duty of loyalty**—the duty to keep the interest of the corporation paramount above personal interests when acting for or on behalf of the corporation.

There are certain activities that the board as a whole may follow in order to ensure that its directors act in accordance with the duties of care and duties of loyalty. These activities include:

- Holding regular meetings.

- Keeping minutes of board and committee meetings.

- Ensuring that all government filings are made on time.

- Selecting, hiring, and removing directors and officers.

- Following the requirements for federal and state tax exempt status.

- Fulfilling the conditions imposed by grant funding sources.

- Approving and managing an annual budget.

- Reviewing the financial audit of the organization.

- Adequately protecting corporate properties and assets with insurance.

- Following the articles of incorporation and bylaws.

---

[2] All material used in this sub-heading was taken from "Ten Commandments of Prudent Activities for a Not-for-Profit Board of Directors," a brochure published by Foley, Hoag & Eliot.

- Monitoring and evaluating the implementation of board policies and decisions.

This list is long, but it doesn't cover everything. Aside from the responsibilities that laws and funders impose on board members, much of what a board decides to do is up to the board itself.

2. Can young people legally serve on a board in my state?

Because each state makes its own laws, you should check to see what the laws are around youth governance in your state. At the end of this chapter you will find a full listing of states and their laws on youth involvement. For the most part, you will find three different kinds of state rulings:

1. A law that says it is legal for young people to serve as directors, with age stipulations.

2. A law stating that it is not legal for young people to vote on boards if they are under a certain age.

3. No law on the issue at all.

Four types of minimal age requirements

When there is an age requirement mentioned in a law, there are several ways it might be written. They include:

Age-specific requirements for directors. When a specific minimum age is named for directors, it means that no one on an organization's board of directors (or other formal governing body, such as a vestry) can be under the given age. It *does not* regulate informal governance bodies like youth advisory councils or non-voting committees.

Age-specific requirements for incorporators. When a specific minimum age is named for an incorporator, it means that the person who is the signatory on articles of incorporation and other legally binding documents cannot be under the given age. It *does not*, however, prevent a young person from founding an organization, as long as she or he is not the legally recognized incorporator of the organization.

No minimum age required. In 43 states there are no minimum age requirements for directors or incorporators.

Age-specific requirements for contractual agreements. In every state there is a minimum age (the age of majority) at which a contract can be said to be binding. All those below this age are considered minors. Although this age requirement does not explicitly refer to the ability of minors to serve on a board of directors, it does become an important issue in considering the liability of the board in the case of a civil action. However, as long as the minor is not the officer authorized to sign on behalf of the organization, or the signatory to the agreement, the minor's inability to contract should not become an issue.

3. When there is no law, what does that mean?

No law means that it has not been proven legal or illegal, so it would be fine for young people to serve on your board. However, as mentioned above, each state has specific laws pertaining to the age that people can enter into legal contracts. Though most board work does not involve making contracts, you should be aware of the contract laws in your state. At Youth on Board, we have researched this question in the Commonwealth of Massachusetts. Our legal counsel drafted a document for our board of directors on this issue so members would have a greater understanding of the matter. In Massachusetts, young people under the age of 18 cannot enter into a legal contract. Here are a few suggestions that pertain to all boards:

• Young people should not be signatories on checking accounts.

- Young people should not sign binding contracts with consultants, businesses, or other entities. This includes documents involved in hiring.

- In matters that involve legal contracts, young people's votes should not break a tie or count to make a majority vote. (See "Recording Votes" chart in this chapter.)

4. How is voting handled with young members on board?

When drafting or amending your own conflict of interest policy, always consult an attorney, since legal guidelines do vary from state to state.

Youth board members act in the capacity in which they have been asked to serve. In terms of voting, there are four ways that youth can serve on a board:

Voting member. This is the most inclusive way to involve young people on a board, as a voting member with full rights and responsibilities. Young people can be elected, hand-picked, or recommended for this position. We strongly suggest that you ask two or three young people to join at one time.

Non-voting member. Another option for youth involvement is to create a position for a youth board member in which they function as a full board member in all ways, *except* that she or he does not have voting power. This option is often used by groups whose board members are concerned about liability issues. Note that it is easy to fall into the trap of tokenism with non-voting youth members. Be sure to include these members in all other aspects of board business.

Observing member. In addition to providing information about the organization's programs and activities, observing gives young people the chance to see what being on a board is all about. Young observers may bring information from board meetings back to a youth advisory board or other entity on which they currently serve, thus improving communication among groups.

Are Young People Covered by Your Organization's Insurance?

It is common for nonprofits to carry what is known as Directors and Organizers (D & O) Insurance for all of its board members. The purpose of this insurance is to protect the board, as well as the founding organizers, from any legal liability. Most policies do not specify a minimum age for board members. Because board members are financially liable for the organization, the board can be sued for breach of duty. D & O Insurance protects against this. In the unfortunate event that a lawsuit is brought against the organization, the insurer will in most cases pay the damages awarded against the board members, as well as the board members' legal fees. Check your policy to make sure that board members who are minors can also be protected by this insurance.

Observing can also serve as a training mechanism for future board members of any age.

Majority youth board. There are some places where it makes good sense for there to be a youth board that stands alone as the governing body. This can be handled in several ways. For instance, an adult or two may also serve on the youth board for advisory purposes. Or, for legal purposes, there may be an adult body that ratifies the official decisions made by the youth board.

5. If the law in my state does not permit young people to vote on boards, how can I work around it?

If your state prohibits the inclusion of youth as full voting board members, there are some things that can be done to include youth in governance. The nonprofit organization Community Partnerships with Youth, Inc., in Fort Wayne, IN, recommends four options for overcoming such legal barriers:

Youth in non-voting positions[3]

Ask young people to take an ex officio or ad hoc position on the board. This means that they participate in discussions, serve on committees, and partake in all board events, but they do not vote. Although most youth wanting to serve on a board also want voting rights, in this case they would not be allowed to do so.

Record votes as youth vs. adult

Have youth join in the discussions, serve on committees, and join all board events, but count the votes differently. All votes are recorded as youth or adult. If the youth vote carries for or against the motion, or breaks a tie, then the board motion or committee decision must fail. For example:

Recording Votes

	Youth	Adult
Yea	3	7
Nay	0	5
Motion Carries		

	Youth	Adult
Yea	3	5
Nay	0	7
Motion Fails		

	Youth	Adult
Yea	3	6
Nay	0	7
Motion Fails		

This option allows youth the chance to vote, but prohibits their vote from carrying a decision. This process sidesteps the issue of whether youth decisions are legally binding.

Youth on board committees

Board committees are advisory groups that usually form to research an issue and then advise the governing body on its findings. Committees are not subject to the laws regarding minors serving on boards. Thus, asking youth to serve on board committees such as fundraising, programs, future planning, or marketing frees the board (and the youth) of the legal snares in which they may otherwise get entangled. It also allows for the youth vote to be an important one: The entire committee votes on a decision and then the

[3] Material in this section was adapted from the Community Partnerships with Youth publication *Youth in Governance: A Board/Committee Member Curriculum.*

board ratifies that decision. In addition, youth can attend the board meetings where committee reports are made, enabling them to gain experience in decision making and meeting etiquette.

Adult advisory board and signatory power

Several groundbreaking organizations have assembled boards of directors that consist entirely of young people. In this case, the legal concerns of contract validity are heightened. In some states, it is not possible for board members to sign a contract when everyone, including the board chair, is under the age of 18.

One possible solution to this dilemma is to create an independent adult advisory board that has signatory power for the organization, acting on decisions made by the all-youth board. While there is currently little legal precedence from which to draw upon, we do applaud organizations willing to take this bold step. They may, in fact, be the ones establishing legal precedents for the future.

STORIES FROM THE STREET

Because of time and effort put in by many concerned individuals in the state of New York, a law was passed in 1983 to ensure that nonprofits geared toward youth involvement also involve youth as board members. The law—proposed and fought for by young people— enables 16- and 17-year-olds to serve as full voting members of boards of directors. The following is an excerpt from this law:

"...a corporation organized for educational purposes primarily for the benefit of individuals below eighteen years of age may include one director below eighteen years of age who is at least sixteen years of age. Further, a corporation organized for recreational or youth development and delinquency prevention purposes primarily for the benefit of individuals below eighteen years of age may include one or more directors, the number of which shall not exceed one-half of the total number of directors for a

quorum for the transaction of business, who are at least sixteen years of age but not over eighteen years of age."

In 1998, a similar bill was passed in the Michigan house by an overwhelming majority of 78 to 10. Many people are to be congratulated for their hard work and effort in making sure that the rights of young people in Michigan are safeguarded. The petition to change the law reads:

Substitute For House Bill No. 5906

A bill to amend 1982 PA 162, entitled "Nonprofit corporation act," (MCL 450.2101 to 450.3192) by adding section 501a.

The People of the State of Michigan Enact:

Sec. 501A. (1) A corporation organized for purposes described in section 501(c)(3) of the internal revenue code of 1986 may include 1 or more directors on its board who are 16 or 17 years of age as long as that number does not exceed the total number of directors required for a quorum for the transaction of business.

(2) If a corporation described in subsection (1) may have more than 1 director who is 16 or 17 years of age, the corporation shall state in its articles of incorporation the number of directors who may be 16 or 17 years of age.

Like the New York law, this law allows a corporate board organized for people under the age of 18 to include directors who are 16 and 17 years old. The passage of this bill is a hopeful sign that, with determination and commitment, no legal barrier is insurmountable for young people and their allies.

How to Change the Law

You too can change your state's laws. As Wendy Schaetzel Lesko, founder of the Activism 2000 Project, and other Project members write, "You don't need to be a top expert or the 'hired gun' of a large company or organization in order to be heard. You don't even need to be of voting age." Nor do you need to completely understand the complex and unpredictable process of legislation in order to make your voice heard. The trick is to find a mentor—someone familiar with the legal process who can help you make your case. This can be a lawyer who serves as legal counsel for your organization, an experienced lobbyist, your own state legislator, or a member of his or her staff.

Before finding a mentor, however, it's best to do a little homework of your own. Since you know that your goal is to create or change existing laws pertaining to the voting age of board members, find out which individuals and agencies in your state wrote the existing law or could support your efforts to change the law. And remember that enlisting support includes alerting your local newspaper and any other relevant publications to what you're doing. Also keep in mind that changing laws takes time, and sometimes money. You may want to delegate to someone the responsibility of researching grants for your initiative.

After developing a strong proposal and finding a mentor, it's time to begin the battle. This process involves, among other legislative tasks, trips to the state house. It can be long, and at times frustrating, but if you are determined to see it through, it promises to be equally exciting.

We note that, while we applaud all states that have laws allowing for young people to vote on boards, we suggest that any laws you create do not specify the ages of youth board members (beyond the statement "below the age of 18"). Who's to say a 17-year-old is more qualified to serve than a 13-year-old? By not specifying an age, your board can determine membership based on the qualifications of anyone they want to have join.

For more information on changing laws, check out the publication *Youth! The 26% Solution*, published by the Activism 2000 Project (1-800-KID-POWER).

A Survey of Minimum Age Requirements by State

The list below specifies the age requirements for youth on boards of nonprofits for the 50 states. Where restrictions also exist for incorporators of organizations, that information is also provided. In order for you to locate the legal documents containing this information, we have included the statutory source(s) regarding each state's requirements for a nonprofit board of directors. If you'd like to examine the laws in your own state, these statutes can be obtained through your own legal counsel or by visiting your local courthouse, state house library, or any law library.

State	Age of Directors and Incorporators	Statutory Source
Alabama	No minimum age for directors specified	ALA. CODE ß 10-3A-34
Alaska	No minimum age for directors specified Incorporators must be 19 or older	ALASKA STAT. ß10.20.081 ALASKA STAT. ß10.20.146
Arizona	No minimum age for directors specified	ARIZ. REV. STAT. ANN. ß 10-2317
Arkansas	No minimum age for directors specified	ARK. CODE ANN. ß 4-33-802
California	No minimum age for directors specified	CAL. CORP. CODE ß 5151(c)(3)
Colorado	No minimum age for directors specified	COLO. REV. STAT. ß 7-24-101
Connecticut	No minimum age for directors specified	CONN. GEN. STAT. ANN ß 33-448
Delaware	No minimum age for directors specified	DEL. CODE ANN tit. 8 ß 141
Florida	Directors must be 18 or older	FLA. STAT. ANN. ß 617.0802.
Georgia	Directors must be 18 or older	GA. CODE ANN. ß 14-2-802
Hawaii	No minimum age for directors specified	HAW. REV. STAT. ß 415B-61
Idaho	No minimum age for directors specified	IDAHO CODE ß 30-3-64
Illinois	No minimum age for directors specified	ILL. REV. STAT. ch. 105 para. 108.05
Indiana	No minimum age for directors specified	IND. CODE ß 23-17-12-2
Iowa	No minimum age for directors specified	IOWA CODE ß 504A.17
Kansas	No minimum age for directors specified	KAN. STAT. ANN ßß 17-6301, 17-6805
Kentucky	No minimum age for directors specified	KY. REV. STAT. ANN. ß 273.207
Louisiana	No minimum age for directors specified	LA. REV. STAT. ANN. ß 12:224
Maine	No minimum age for directors specified	ME. REV. STAT. ANN. Tit. 13-b, ß 701
Maryland	No minimum age for directors specified	MD. CODE ANN., CORP. ß 2-403
Mass.	No minimum age for directors specified Incorporators must be 18 or older	MASS. GEN. LAWS ANN. ch. 180, ß 6C MASS. GEN. LAWS ANN. ch. 180, ß 3
Michigan	For corporations for youth education, recreation, or development, directors must be 16 or over	MICH. COMP. LAWS ANN. ß 450.2501
Minnesota	Majority of the directors must be adults	MINN. STAT. ß 317A.205

Mississippi	No minimum age for directors	MISS. CODE ANN. ß 79-11-101
Missouri	No minimum age for directors specified Incorporators must be 18 or older	MO. REV. STAT. ß 355.130 MO. REV. STAT. ß 355.040
Montana	No minimum age for directors specified	MONT. CODE ANN. ß 35-2-415
Nebraska	No minimum age for directors specified	NEB. REV. STAT. ß 21-1916
Nevada	Directors must be 18 or older	NEV. REV. STAT. ß 82.196
New Hamp.	No minimum age for directors specified	N.H. REV. STAT. ANN. ßßß 292:1, 293-A:8.02, 293-A:2.01
New Jersey	Trustees must be 18 or older	N.J. REV. STAT. ß 15A:6-1
New Mexico	No minimum age for directors specified	N.M. STAT. ANN. ß 53-8-17
New York	For corporations for youth education, recreation, or development, directors must be 16 or over	N.Y. CORPORATIONS LAW ß 701
No. Car.	No minimum age for directors specified	N.C. GEN. STAT. ß 55A-8-02
No. Dak.	No minimum age for directors specified	N.D. CENT. CODE ß 10-24-17
Ohio	No minimum age for directors specified	OHIO REV. CODE ANN. ß 1702.27(3)
Oklahoma	No minimum age for directors specified	OKLA. STAT. ANN. tit. 18, ß 1027
Oregon	No minimum age for directors specified Incorporators must be 18 or older	OR. REV. STAT. ß 65.304 OR. REV. STAT. ß 65.044
Penn.	Directors must be "of full age," defined as 18 or older Rhode Island No minimum age for directors specified	15 PA. CONS. STAT. ANN ßß 5722, 5103 R.I. GEN. LAWS ß 7-6-22(a)
So. Car.	No minimum age for directors specified	S.C. CODE ANN. ß 33-31-802
So. Dak.	No minimum age for directors specified Incorporators must be of the age of majority	S.D. CODIFIED LAWS ANN. ß 47-23-13 S.D. CODIFIED LAWS ANN. ß 47-22-5
Tennessee	No minimum age for directors specified	TENN. CODE ANN. ß 44-58-102
Texas	No minimum age for directors specified Incorporators must be 18 or older	TEX. CIV. STAT. CODE ANN. ß 1392-2.14 TEX. CIV. STAT. CODE ANN. ß 1396-3.01
Utah	No minimum age for directors specified	UTAH CODE ANN. ß 16-10a-802
Vermont	No minimum age for directors specifiedI Incorporators must be of the age of majority	VT. STAT. ANN. tit. 11 ß 2364 VT. STAT. ANN. tit. 11 ß 2401
Virginia	No minimum age for directors specified	VA. CODE ANN. ß 13.1-854
Washington	No minimum age for directors specified Incorporators must be 18 or older	WASH. REV. CODE ANN. ß 24.03.095 WASH. REV. CODE ANN. ß 24.03.020
W. Va.	No minimum age for directors specified	W. VA. CODE ß 31-1-139
Wisconsin	No minimum age for directors specified Incorporators must be 18 or older	WIS. STAT. ANN. ß 181.18 WIS. STAT. ANN. ß 181.30
Wyoming	No minimum age for directors specified	WYO. STAT. ß 17-19-802

6

Legal Language

Use this worksheet as you read through this chapter on overcoming legal barriers. Jot down words or phrases that you don't understand. And as others read this chapter, or have questions about legal terms, encourage them to write on this same list. Once all terms are defined, share this list with your entire group so that everyone has the same information. We have started the list by defining a few terms for you. Consult a dictionary, law library, or legal mentor to help you define additional terms.

Term	Definition
Ad hoc	For a specific purpose, case, or situation.*
Agreement	A properly executed and legally binding document.*
Assets	A valuable item that is owned.*
Contract	An agreement between two or more parties, especially one that is written and enforceable by law.*
Duty of Care	The duty to perform responsibilities in good faith and in a manner that is reasonably believed to be in the best interests of a corporation, and with such care as an ordinarily prudent person in a like position with respect to a similar corporation would use in similar circumstances.
Duty of Loyalty	The duty to keep the interest of the corporation paramount above personal interests when acting for or on behalf of a corporation.
Ex officio	By virtue of office or position.* For example, an organization's bylaws may state that the executive director is automatically a member of the board.
Incorporator	One who legally forms a corporation.*
Liable	Legally obligated or responsible.*
Signatory Power	Having the authority to sign a document in order for that document to have legality.

Additional Terms:

* Definitions taken from the 1982 *The American Heritage Dictionary Second College Edition.*

Recruit Young People

This chapter offers a tangible process for creating and implementing a strong recruitment program.

The search is on! Your board, advisory council, vestry, or other governing body wants to find a young decision maker —or better yet, several. But who to choose?

As you may know from recruiting adults, at least half of the success of creating a great board depends upon your recruitment process. For example, if you want a corporate, money-connected board and you are able to recruit the CEO of the largest local business in your area, you've done well. Likewise, if you want to have an organization that involves young people in a significant way, you must recruit from among those young people who believe in your cause and will help you meet your objectives.

As you enter this process, think about the implications of your strategy. Some organizations recruit the top people and then find that they are too busy to do any board work or attend meetings. Others recruit individuals with lots of time but few connections or little clout.

When choosing a young person to work with your organization, most important is finding someone who possesses motivation, a unique perspective, and a readiness for your governance environment. You will likely find that word-of-mouth advertising goes a long way in connecting you to potential board members. Don't hesitate to solicit names from young people that you, members of your staff and your council, board, or task force already know. However, when recruiting through other people, make it clear that you are not looking just for the "stars." Watch out for over-committed youth who may have little time to give to the organization.

By following the basic techniques and goals outlined in this section, you're certain to recruit the best possible young decision maker(s) for your governing body. Note that these same techniques can be used with equal success for recruiting adult members.

Steps for Effective Recruiting

Follow these steps as you work toward obtaining the young people (or any member) you want join your governance structure:

1. Be clear about what you want.

2. Define your selection process.

3. Recruit candidates and review expectations.

4. Select candidate(s).

5. Notify those accepted and rejected.

6. Evaluate your strategy.

7. Document the process.

1. Be clear about what you want [1]

As with any strong team, a governing body should reflect an even balance of interest, skills, and diversity among its members. There are some characteristics that are important for every member of your governing body to possess, and some skills that only a few members need to have. When recruiting new members, it is commonly said that all members should offer two of three criteria: work, wealth, or wisdom. Members should be able to put sweat equity into your effort, contribute money, or offer important perspectives and advice. When recruiting young people, remember

[1] Information in this section was taken from the Support Center's for Non-Profit Management/National Minority AIDS Council's *Action Handbook for Boards.*

that age is not the only criteria—never choose a young person to be a group member just because he or she is young.

Before selecting new members, consider creating a governing body profile—a simple list of characteristics already found in the group, as well as those skills you hope new members will possess. (Use the "Board Profile" worksheet at the end of this chapter to help you.) Every governing body requires some common characteristics among board members that will contribute to their function in the group. They include a commitment to the organization and its mission, and a willingness to fulfill obligations of the group and participate in the work of the group. What other skills should your governance group possess? Some possible answers include the following:

- **Specialized skills:** One or two members may be knowledgeable about a particular subject, such as a financial or legal background.

- **Diversity:** Members should reflect the various ages, races, economic and religious backgrounds, genders, and sexual orientations of the client population and constituency of the organization.

- **Community affiliations:** Members who are well-connected can share their contacts with the organization.

- **Understanding of field:** If your work is specialized, it may be helpful to find members who understand your field.

The following qualities apply to all members you want to recruit, but should be particularly sought after in young people:

- **Readiness for the environment:** Working in a governance position requires one to be prepared to work with many different kinds of people.

• **Confidence and outspokenness:** Whenever working with groups of people, one must be assertive in order to be heard.

• **Readiness for responsibility:** It is often tempting to reach out to young people who you think "should be on a board," or who you want to help. While well-intentioned, this is not an effective selection policy. The governing body is not a place for young people who need lots of extra attention because this work requires a team effort. Challenge the stereotype that a governing leader must be an adult, but also choose someone who is ready for the position.

• **Willingness to work:** To be a contributing member, a young person must be active and ready to take on special projects or join committees.

• **Motivation for the job:** They should be passionate about the cause for which they are working.

• **Connections with other youth:** It is particularly useful if young leaders are well connected to other youth who can provide them with a broader perspective and can recruit others to volunteer for your organization.

Now that you've established the criteria that are important to you and your governing body, it's time to set up a recruitment process that will attract the right people.

2. Define your recruitment process

It is important to keep in mind your timeframe, financial resources, personnel, and other organizational concerns when developing a recruitment process. Here are four options—along with possible drawbacks of each—that you may want to consider as you develop a recruitment process strategy:

Recommendations and referrals

Many boards hand pick individuals who they think would be strong candidates. This process allows staff or board members who know qualified young people to collect resumes or bios of potential applicants. If you have a selection committee, they would then review applicants and present the best candidates to the full board for approval.

Caution: This option may not allow for a large selection of applicants to be considered.

It may also invite nepotism and personal bias.

Open selection

If you make an open call for applicants by, for example, advertising in your local high school newspaper, you can open up your process to a wide range of youth. This is a wonderful way to educate a wide audience about, and gain much exposure for, your organization. You can also use this process as an opportunity to educate young people about your board and governance process. Provide an orientation or training session for all interested young people and then take them through an interview process.

Caution: This process takes time, both in collecting information and during the actual screening of applicants.

Nomination of alumni

You may want to call for applicants among young people who have been previously involved with your program in some way. This strategy ensures that you have some preexisting knowledge about the young person's commitment, skill level, and interests.

Caution: This option does not allow for input or perspective from people outside of your organization.

Nomination by youth

If you already have a group of young people connected to your organization, think about asking them to select other young people to be considered for membership on your governance structure. Help them set up rules and a process for selection and let them go from there. This works best if young people are trained in what it means to be a board member. Remind them that the board has final say about selection.

Caution: If young people don't understand the job, this process could turn into a popularity contest among them. Be sure to carefully check the credentials of the young people nominated, and be clear about job expectations.

Nominating committee

Once you decide how you want to recruit board or committee members, you may want to establish a nominating committee to carry out the process. In addition to providing a focus for the task, a committee can be a great way to involve your board, advisory council, or church vestry in the process of finding a new member. It can also lighten the workload for staff people. When forming a nominating committee, there are several questions to consider, including: Do you want this group to be a long-term nominating body or a temporary group? Who should be on the committee? Do you want to involve non-governing board members on the committee? Is there a staff person, a current young person not eligible for the board, or a close friend of the organization that should be an advisor in this process?

3. Recruit candidates

Youth-serving organizations naturally have greater access to young people than organizations that do not have youth as a constituent population. This does not necessarily mean, however, that they will have an easier time finding a young person for their governing body.

Encourage young people who know your group well to share a good word with their peers.

Don't overlook the obvious when recruiting—encourage young people who know your group well to share a good word with their peers. This is the best way to get the word out. Also, talk to adults who are in regular contact with young people. Teachers, youth workers, ministers, and parents are a great place to start. Following are more suggestions on where and how to look:

- Hold group outreach programs at the beginning of a recruitment process to let a broad range of young people understand what you are doing and why. At Youth on Board, we strongly recommend this method. It is a good, non-threatening way to invite young people into the process. It can also be used to introduce them to governance in general. Make group outreach programs fun, interactive, and informative. An interview will go into detail, so don't go over everything now. Just provide enough information to get people excited and informed about how to apply.

- Ask community leaders to suggest a candidate.

- Place an ad in a local paper, newsletter, or youth publication.

- During presentations and conversations, mention your need for new members.

- Contact student clubs and faculty members at local high schools and colleges.

- Place advertisements on web sites frequented by young people.

- Post flyers at community centers, corner stores, coffee shops, and other youth hang-outs.

Be sure to give young people specific and detailed information about expectations of board members, times and locations of meetings, and reasons they may want to apply. Use the worksheet at the end of this chapter to create a job description, and go over it with anyone interested in the position.

4. Select candidate(s)

There are many ways to conduct selection sessions. Again, think about your needs and your resources. Consider the following options and then decide which strategy makes the most sense for your organization:

One-on-one interview

Often an organization will set up recruitment and selection committees to conduct one-on-one interviews with potential members. (See the "Sample Agenda" at the end of the chapter.)

Group interviews

Group interviews, as an alternative to one-on-one interviews, enable you to see how young people interact in a group setting. Group interviews can occur when a group of members interview one candidate, or several candidates at once. In addition, it may be logistically easier to schedule one meeting where all current board members can interview board applicants.

Telephone interviews

If you can't get people together in person, you may want to conduct phone interviews. Phone interviews are excellent for screening applicants prior to face-to-face interviews. Remember, while these can be valuable, there is nothing like meeting candidates in person.

Paper selection

If you don't have enough time or staff to conduct telephone or in-person interviews, your last viable option is to make recommendations based on documents. You might require candidates to submit a written application, recommendations, and a sample of something that they have created or written. This is not the best option, because it is easier to explain expectations and measure a young person's comprehension of the job in person.

Recommendations

Recommendations can be used as a primary means for selecting candidates, or as a supplement to other methods of selection. It makes sense, however, to research on your own in addition to basing decisions on the recommendations of others. Remember that you can use both written recommendations and phone recommendations.

5. Notify those accepted and rejected

Once you have selected your new board member(s), you'll want to inform all applicants of your decisions.

Acceptance

Give young people a call and let them know that they've been accepted.

During the acceptance phone call, be sure to remind new members of any upcoming meetings or events. Also be sure to set up an orientation meeting.

After the phone call, follow up with an official letter outlining their role and again reminding them about upcoming events or meetings. The letter can be a standard acceptance letter, or you may consider sending a Letter of Agreement, which is explained in *Point 8: Create a Strong Orientation Process*.

Send them the "I've Just Been Nominated to a Board" form located at the end of *Point 8*. Also send news articles about your organization, or any other general information you want your new member to have.

Rejection

Remember that it is a big deal for most young people to even think about taking on a leadership role, so be gentle in letting them know that they have not been selected. Always speak directly to the candidate rather than sending something through the mail, or leaving a message. Let them know their strengths, and tell them exactly what you were looking for so they know what they might work on developing for the future. Be sure to thank them for applying, and offer encouragement for finding another opportunity for a leadership role, either within your organization or with another. If you know of any specific options, let them know.

6. Evaluate your strategy

Evaluate the positive and negative aspects of your recruitment and selection processes. An easy way to do this is to brainstorm the pluses and minuses with your group and marking each down in columns on a sheet of paper or on a flip chart. This is likely to be the first of many recruitment efforts for young people, so use it as an opportunity for learning. Remember that you are just starting and you can't expect perfection. What is most important is that you have made the effort, and that future efforts can only get better.

7. Document your process

Because this probably won't be the last time you recruit new youth members, it is important to leave a paper trail. Create a binder or have the nomination committee write a memo to summarize their process and their findings. It's helpful to compile lists of people contacted, phone numbers, e-mail addresses, etc., so that next time you can start from there, rather than from scratch. You might even have the new youth members write about their perspective of the process. Build on this paper trail each time you have a recruitment and selection process.

Always speak directly to the candidate rather than sending something through the mail, or leaving a message.

Youth Express[2] is an organization that runs various youth programs in the Lexington-Hamline neighborhood of St. Paul, MN. It was founded in the neighborhood and recruits young people, mainly by word of mouth, from youth and their parents. They announce events, programs, and job opportunities for youth in their local newspaper, and in their own organizational newsletter. One of the best ways they recruit is to ask young people what they are interested in, and if it doesn't already exist, they help them start it.

Adult staff at Youth Express also work with the city's school Truancy Intervention Program (TIP) to recruit young people that are having a hard time in school. Young people with truancy problems are referred to Youth Express and are encouraged to get involved in community projects and programs. The TIP staff has seen an improvement in school attendance directly linked to the student's involvement with Youth Express. Youth Express ensures that it is not just working with self-identified young leaders, but also with young people with many different needs and interests.

7

[2] Youth Express, 168 North Griggs Street, St. Paul, MN 55104. Phone: 651/659-0613.

Job Description

Use this worksheet as a guide to creating a job description for youth board members.

Title:

Competencies or characteristics we are looking for:

Responsibilities:

Time commitment:

Travel commitment:

Special needs, events, requirements:

58 Day Street, P.O. Box 440322, Somerville, MA 02144 • 617.623.9900 x1242

Perquisites (will young people get to travel, meet community leaders, etc.?):

Training:

Reimbursements:

Other:

Sample Interview Agenda

This sample, developed from the National Center for Nonprofit Board publication Six Keys to Recruiting, Orienting, and Involving Nonprofit Board Members, *is designed for a one-on-one interview, but can easily be adapted for a group interview.*

Introduction:

• Thank the candidate for meeting with you.

• Explain that while you are meeting with the candidate individually to provide a recommendation, the governance body will be making the final decision, if that is your decision process.

About your organization and its governing body:

• Explain your connection with the organization.

• Explain the mission, history, and programs of your organization. Ask whether the candidate has any questions.

• Explain why you are interested in the person as a prospective member. Be specific, naming skills you admire in that person. Also state whether or not you have previously had young people on your board.

• Explain what the governance position entails. Include how much time members are expected to commit, how many meetings there are per year, and any annual contribution expectations.

• Mention if there is a mentoring or a "buddy system" in place.

• Review the letter of agreement (which is essentially a contract for the job, and provides an opportunity for you to specify what is expected of a board member).

• Explain what training is provided.

• Explain some of the critical issues currently facing the board.

• Explain voting rights of young board members.

• Explain the reimbursement policy for travel expenses.

Questions for the candidate:

- Why are you interested in this organization? What aspect of our mission or work is most appealing to you?

- What kind of commitment are you able to make to the organization?

- Why are you interested in joining our governance group?

- What is your background and experience? What kind of service have you done?

- What skills, training, resources, and expertise do you have to offer? What are you hoping to contribute and to gain?

- What do you consider to be your weaknesses?

- What can the organization do to help you be successful as a leader or member of a governing body?

Closing:

- Ask whether the candidate is still interested in the position.

- Invite the candidate to observe a meeting, event, or one of the organization's programs.

- If the candidate declines the nomination, ask whether she or he wants to serve the organization in another capacity, such as volunteer, donor, advisor, or provider of in-kind goods or services.

- Offer a packet of information about the organization and its governance. (Do not give materials to the candidate at the beginning of the meeting, so as not to distract her or him.)

WORKSHEET

Board Profile

Use this worksheet to help you determine what characteristics your governing body currently possesses, and what you should seek in recruiting additional members. The contents of this worksheet was adapted from Six Keys to Recruiting, Orienting and Involving Nonprofit Board Members *by Judith Grummon Nelson. Please note that each number represents the name of a current board member, and each letter represents the name of a prospective board member.*

Categories to Consider	Current Board Members				Prospective Board Members			
Area of expertise/ professional skills	1	2	3	4	A	B	C	D
Organizational and financial management								
Special program focus of our nonprofit (e.g. education, health, public policy, etc.)								
Administration								
Business/corporate								
Finance: Accounting Banking and trusts Investments								
Fundraising								
Government regulations								
Law								
Marketing								
Personnel								
Physical plant (architect, engineer)								
Strategic or long-range planning								
Public relations								
Real estate								
Representative of clients served by nonprofit								
Youth issues								
Counseling								
Other								

continued on next page

Categories to Consider		Current Board Members				Prospective Board Members			
personal characteristics		1	2	3	4	A	B	C	D
Ages:	Under 35								
	From 35 to 50								
	From 51 to 65								
	Over 65								
Gender:	Women								
	Men								
Physical disability									
Sexual orientation									
Race/ethnic background:									
	Asian/Pacific Islander								
	Black/African American								
	Hispanic/Latino								
	Native American								
	Caucasian								
	Other								
Geographical location (depending on your mission):									
	City								
	Suburbs								
	State								
	Regional								
	National								
	International								
Financial position:	Self-employed								
	Salaried								
	Philanthropic reputation								
	Prospective major donor								
	Student								

POINT
NUMBER

8

Create a Strong Orientation Process

This chapter outlines the importance of providing an orientation for new youth board members, and gives an overview of several tools that can assist in that process.

Helping young people feel comfortable in their new leadership position is critical to their success on the board. In order for this to happen, they will need information, supportive relationships, and a clear sense of their role in the organization. A solid orientation process can help further these goals.

Most strong boards already have some form of orientation for all board members. If this is the case for your group, this work will be easier for you. If you don't yet have a thorough orientation process in place, take this opportunity to create an orientation that will benefit both youth and adults.

Effective Orientation

There are four parts of an effective orientation that we advise all groups to implement. They include:

1. Create a letter of agreement: A letter documenting the expectations and responsibilities of the new member.

2. Host an orientation session: A meeting to review roles and allow new members to share their concerns, questions, and excitement. (A guide for topics and sample handouts are included at the end of this chapter.)

3. Create ongoing orientation: Periodic check-ins with new members during the first couple of months to answer questions and hear concerns. This may also happen as part of a board mentoring program.

4. Conduct a parental orientation: A discussion, by phone or in person, with the young person's parents to review the scope of responsibilities and schedule of board activities, as well as an opportunity to hear their concerns and questions.

The following pages review recommendations for creating each of these orientation processes.

1. Create a letter of agreement

A letter of agreement clarifies the role of each member on the governing body and the responsibilities of the organization, and also establishes a formal relationship between the two.

We recommend that every group have a standard letter of agreement and that you do two things with it. First, go over the letter of agreement step-by-step with new members. You can do this during a one-on-one conversation or during an orientation session. Second, a designated staff or board member and the young person should sign the letter. This gives it extra weight and helps young people understand that they are committing to a clear set of expectations and responsibilities.

A letter of agreement should include: key expectations of the job of board member, advisory board member, etc.; important commitments, either of time or travel; and ways in which the organization, city office, church, or other entity will support the young person in his or her new role. At the end of this chapter, we have included a sample letter of agreement you may want to adopt for your own group.

2. Host an orientation session

We can't emphasize enough that, if young people are to thrive in their positions, they need support and information early in their role as board members. Getting off to a bad start can set progress back for months.

So, what does a good orientation session look like? It should be a balance of fun and information. Begin with an ice-breaker, such as asking everyone to introduce and describe his or herself in two sentences, so that everyone feels comfortable and relaxed. Then help them feel ownership of your committee, board, or council by explaining exactly how the work they do affects your organization. An orientation session is also a good time to go over the letter of agreement and review important dates. There is a worksheet at the end of this chapter that lists various orientation topics. Whatever you choose to include, make the orientation as interactive as possible.

There are many ways to present important information in a fun way. Be creative. For example, give some basic information about the history and mission of your group by engaging young people in a game. Make up cards with questions on them, each worth 14 points (we couldn't resist!). After you have handed out a fact sheet on the organization and given participants a few minutes to review it, ask questions from the sheet and award point cards for each correct answer. The person with the most points can win something simple, like a company pen. And consider these additional ideas: instead of listing their roles, facilitate a brainstorming session and pull ideas from young people. What do they think their responsibilities might include? Rather than go on and on about the organization's missions and goals, why not design a tour or a scavenger hunt where young people have to collect significant information about what your group does? For more on how to create an interactive agenda, see *Point 11: Make Meetings Work*.

3. Create ongoing orientation

Ongoing orientation requires organizations to formally address questions and concerns as they emerge. It is important, especially during the first month or two of a board experience, for young people to know there is a system in place to help them along.

Putting a mentoring structure in place right away is the most appropriate approach to ongoing orientation. In the absence of mentoring, you may want to schedule a second orientation session shortly after the first board meeting. At this point, there are likely to be lots of questions and a new level of both excitement and apprehension among youth participants. At a second orientation session, you might ask young people:

- What did you like about the first meeting?

- What surprised you about the first meeting?

- What did you wish would happen but didn't?

- Is there anything you didn't understand?

- If you were running the meeting, what would you do differently?

These questions give young people permission to voice some of the concerns they may have about their role and expectations. (For a full list of questions to discuss after meetings, see the mentoring worksheet in *Point 12: Develop a Mentoring Plan.*)

We also recommend making individual phone calls to each young person following the first meeting. It is good to check in with them personally regarding their questions, concerns, and impressions.

4. Conduct a parental orientation

In addition to conducting an in-depth orientation with young people, it is very important to help their parents or guardians feel comfortable with your organization as well. Parents play an important role in the success of your young board member. They are often the ones who drive young people to meetings, offer attendance permission when you have a board retreat, and support their child's efforts and achievements. Establishing a relationship early on may prevent problems and misunderstandings down the road.

Putting a mentoring structure in place right away is the most appropriate approach to ongoing orientation.

Some Important Reminders for Adults

What we all want when we sit on a board is to feel like our time is being well spent. We want to feel that we are needed and significant. Young people need to be reminded that what they have to say and who they are is important. Encourage them to voice their opinions in meetings. Remind them that their thoughts and their involvement are important to the group. You can't emphasize these points enough!

Also remember, it is easy for young people to feel overwhelmed by the bulk of information they are getting about their new position. Introduce them to new concepts, systems, people, and information over time. As you look over the "Orientation Checklist" worksheet at the end of this chapter, pick out four or five of the most important topics you think need to be covered first. Allow young people breathing room to absorb the new information before giving them additional layers of information.

Parents or guardians should know at least one individual from your group. It may be a staff person, board mentor, or the chair of the board. Whoever it is, this person needs to take an active role in checking in with parents. For consistency, it should be the same person each time.

If you are planning an orientation with parents, either on the phone or in person, you should cover the following areas: expectations of the youth board members; time commitment and length of term on the board or committee; travel needs; special needs or concerns, such as school schedule, dietary needs, transportation, emotional needs, etc.; and general questions.

"The first time we selected youth board members, I didn't even consider contacting their parents," said Maura Wolf, former director of Boston Do Something[1]. "The young people were in high school, and acted like they were in charge of their lives. Halfway into the year, two youth board members got grounded because of their low school grades, and had to leave the board. I didn't even know they were struggling.

"A year later, one of the same young people asked to join the board again. This time, I got on the phone and talked with his mother. She said he was still struggling with school, but it would be okay for him to rejoin the board because it was such a positive thing in his life. I asked if inviting him to come to the office an hour early on board meeting days to study would be helpful. She said it would be great. Within three months, he was in the office twice a week doing homework before and after board responsibilities. By talking with his mother from the beginning, we got our star young board member back and he was able to stay involved. In addition, his mother became one of our strongest advocates. That experience taught me that if you're working with young people, you're also working with parents!"

---

[1] See the *Resource Directory*, located at the end of this book, for Do Something contact information.

Sample Letter of Agreement

Use this worksheet to help you create a letter of agreement between your organization and new board members.

Agency X's mission statement:

Agency X expects the following from each member:

• Basic Commitment of _____ year(s) and _____ hour(s) per week.

• Attend one meeting every month.

• Be available and eager to represent Agency X in various settings.

• Work to enhance Agency X's public image.

• Work with staff, fellow board members, and program sites to define and monitor the implementation of our mission, goals, and values.

• Help assure fiscal solvency and adequacy of financial resources. Additionally, each member must take an active role in planning and approving the budget and in planning fundraising efforts to meet that budget.

• Actively assist and advise Agency X in the areas of program development and management.

• Serve on a minimum of one committee. Perfect attendance is expected at these meetings.

• Understand the legal responsibilities of the governance body.

What members may expect from Agency X :

• Respectful use of your time.

• Getting important information in a timely manner.

• An interesting, exciting, and valuable experience.

This member's term will be from _____ **to** _____ .

Signature of Member _____

Signature of Director _____

Date _____

Orientation Checklist

Use this checklist as a guide for creating an orientation that is helpful for new members of any age. Remember, less experienced members might require a more detailed orientation that emphasizes basic board operations.

KEY

Yes =   We do this already, and don't need to take further action
N/A =   This is not applicable to us
To consider =   We want to move forward in this area or have questions about whether this applies to us

Yes	N/A	To consider	
☐	☐	☐	Mission of your organization
☐	☐	☐	History of the organization
☐	☐	☐	Names and explanations of all programs
☐	☐	☐	Organizational infrastructure (e.g., names of supervisors, organizational chart, etc.)
☐	☐	☐	Personnel policies
☐	☐	☐	Information on the field in general (e.g., acronyms and jargon)
☐	☐	☐	Meeting protocol (e.g., adding items to the agenda, decision making, etc.)
☐	☐	☐	Attendance policies
☐	☐	☐	Review of bylaws and procedure manuals
☐	☐	☐	Ongoing training offered to members
☐	☐	☐	List of current members with brief biographies
☐	☐	☐	Relevant committee information, including names, descriptions, and current members
☐	☐	☐	Strategic plan, including current successes, struggles, and plans for the future
☐	☐	☐	Internal and external politics (e.g., relationship between your local program and your national program or relationship between your program and the city government or public schools)
☐	☐	☐	Terms of members, systems for nomination, resignation, and replacement
☐	☐	☐	Past and present financial reports and budget information
☐	☐	☐	Board/staff relationships and responsibilities
☐	☐	☐	Community involvement and relationships, including history and political issues
☐	☐	☐	Current unresolved issues within the organization and on the governing body
☐	☐	☐	Relationships with major funders
☐	☐	☐	Sources of current funding and the governing body's role in fundraising
☐	☐	☐	Affirmative action plan and diversity initiatives
☐	☐	☐	Review letter of agreement for new members, stating expectations and responsibilities

Sample Involvement Questionnaire

It is important to have easy access to the credentials and interests of decision makers in your organization. As a specific task or issue arises, you can then turn to an involvement questionnaire to determine who would offer the best skills for the job at hand. Involvement questionnaires are also an excellent medium for organizing basic information about your members and documenting their reasons for being involved with your organization. Use this sample to create an involvement questionnaire for your organization. In addition to the general questions listed below, you can add questions specific to the needs of your organization. Once you know what questions you want to ask, create a questionnaire of your own and distribute it to members.

Name: _____

Occupation/Title: _____

Home Address: _____

Work Address: _____

Home Phone: (   ) _____ Work Phone: (   ) _____

Fax: (   ) _____ E-mail: _____

Best time and place to reach you: _____

Best times for meetings to be scheduled: _____

Please list previous boards, committees, or advisory groups on which you have served and dates served:

List other leadership positions or accomplishments and dates served:

List schools attended or attending (including high school, undergraduate, graduate, and doctoral studies), area of study (as applicable), and date (or anticipated date) of graduation:

List publications, awards, or honors:

List any skills you bring to this group:

Describe your primary reason for joining this group:

List anything else you would like us to know about you:

Tips for Youth Board Members from Youth Board Members

These tips are helpful to young people who serve on boards or other bodies with adults. They were developed by young people who have been in these positions and know the pressures involved.

1. You belong on the board!

You might feel inexperienced at first, or you may think that the adults don't want to hear what you have to say. Remember that your opinions are key to the work the board is doing. As a young person, you have a right and responsibility to be on the board. Young people are part of their communities, and organizations need to hear from them.

2. Find allies.

Find people on the staff and the board who seem to take young people seriously. Sit next to them at meetings, have lunch with them, or talk to them during breaks. When you forget that your role in the group is important, they can help remind you.

3. Ask questions.

If you don't understand something, make sure to ask someone. Your questions are important. You need to understand what's going on, and it won't help anyone if you sit quietly without understanding certain discussions. There will be times when you will feel shy or not interested in what's going on. No matter how you're feeling, it's important to ask questions so you can stay involved.

4. Build a support base for yourself.

Find three young friends who are interested in what you're doing on the board. Talk to them openly about what frustrates you, excites you, or bores you about your work. Choose good listeners who can help you think things through and get some of your feelings out.

5. Get the word out about your leadership.

You have a responsibility to get the word out about the importance of youth leadership to as many young people as possible. It's not just about serving on your board. It's about giving other young people information they can use to take charge. If you're on a foundation board, or any kind of board where you can influence grant policies, encourage the board to fund those organizations that have young people in their governance structures.

6. Know that you are not alone.

There are many young people out there on boards, advisory boards, student councils, etc., working to make a difference in how things are done. You may sometimes feel that the work of your board isn't important. Connecting with other youth board members can help remind you that there is a youth voice movement going on and you're part of it. You can contact the nonprofit youth empowerment agency Youth on Board at 617/623-9900 x1242 to find out about active youth in your area, or just ask around.

7. If you're feeling bored, take responsibility for making board work interesting.

Learn the language of the board or of the organization (e.g., acronyms and jargon). Ask the questions you need to ask. Say at least two things at every board meeting, so you always stay engaged in what's going on. If you feel that meetings need to be jazzed up, suggest something different to do, like brainstorming or small group activities. Chances are other people will also be more engaged if meetings are more interactive.

8. If you don't like how something is going, change it.

You are a member of the group. If you don't think the agenda is interactive enough or you don't like your committee assignment, speak up and work with people to make changes. This may not be easy. You may have to talk it through with people a few times to win them over.

9. Don't get discouraged.

If it feels like people aren't listening or are disrespectful, keep trying. Change usually takes time.

Try to notice when adults do listen and try to understand your thoughts. If you feel like someone is talking down to you, don't be quiet about it. Bring it up. The group needs to deal with the issue.

10. Go to all meetings.

Find out the dates, and write them all down in your calendar. Be prepared for meetings. Read the materials and learn about how things work.

11. Join a committee and take on leadership.

Get involved in the work that happens outside of meetings, and make your presence known. Most work doesn't happen in full meetings, especially on boards of directors. Committees are places where relationships are built and where you can make an even bigger contribution.

12. Relax, have fun, and be yourself.

If you are someone who tells a lot of jokes, then tell jokes. You are a member of the governing body, and you should show who you really are. Think of the other people in the group as your peers.

13. Appreciate adults allies.

Recognize that adults are trying their best, even if things aren't going well. Resist the temptation to criticize.

I've Just Been Nominated to a Board!

What Do I Do?

You're a young person and you've just been nominated to a board. You'll likely be flattered when a representative from Agency X calls to say, "I've nominated you to serve on the board" or "I think you'd be a great board member. Are you interested?" Before committing yourself to anything, you should put some thought into whether or not it makes sense in your life. Consider these questions:

What does the organization do, and am I interested?

It's flattering to be asked to serve on a board. The organization recognizes that you have something valuable to contribute. However, you should investigate whether or not you are interested in what the organization does. The organization may be focused on homelessness when you are interested in HIV and AIDS work. Don't say yes just because you've been asked. Think about what you can learn as well as what you can contribute.

What is the process for joining the board?

We have heard of potential board members who were asked if they were interested in serving on the board and then found themselves listed on the agency letterhead as a board member the very next week. No matter how desperate the agency is for a new member, you should have ample time to ask questions and decide whether or not you want to serve. If there is no interview process in place, ask for one. It is important for both parties to go through an interview process in order for intelligent decisions to be made on both sides.

What is the exact job or the position? What is expected of me?

Are you being asked to be on the board of directors? Board of advisors? Youth council? You need to find out. Each governing body has different responsibilities and jobs. Most boards have a set expectations of time and financial commitments members are expected to make. How many meetings are there? How much money do you have to give or raise on your own? How long are you expected to serve on the board? How do you resign if you don't want to serve on the board? Be sure to ask all relevant questions about your new position.

What is the board like?

What are the board meetings like? Take a look at agendas and minutes from past meetings. Ask to see the board bylaws. These will give you a sense of how the board functions. Also find out who else

58 Day Street, P.O. Box 440322, Somerville, MA 02144 • 617.623.9900 x1242

is on the board. Are there any other young people? Were there young people on the board in the past? Do board members have good relationships with one another? What is the staff like?

Who can help if I have questions?
Where can I go for support?

If this is the first time you've served on a board, you may have a lot of questions. Questions are good! Now, who can you go to with questions? The board chair? The director? Find out who your key contact person is. You may not have enough money for transportation to get to meetings. You may need access to office equipment if you want to make copies of things you've written, or create new documents on a computer. You may want some additional training or an orientation to the organization. If there is not a formal orientation process in place, get someone to sit with you and answer your questions. This is not an outrageous request.

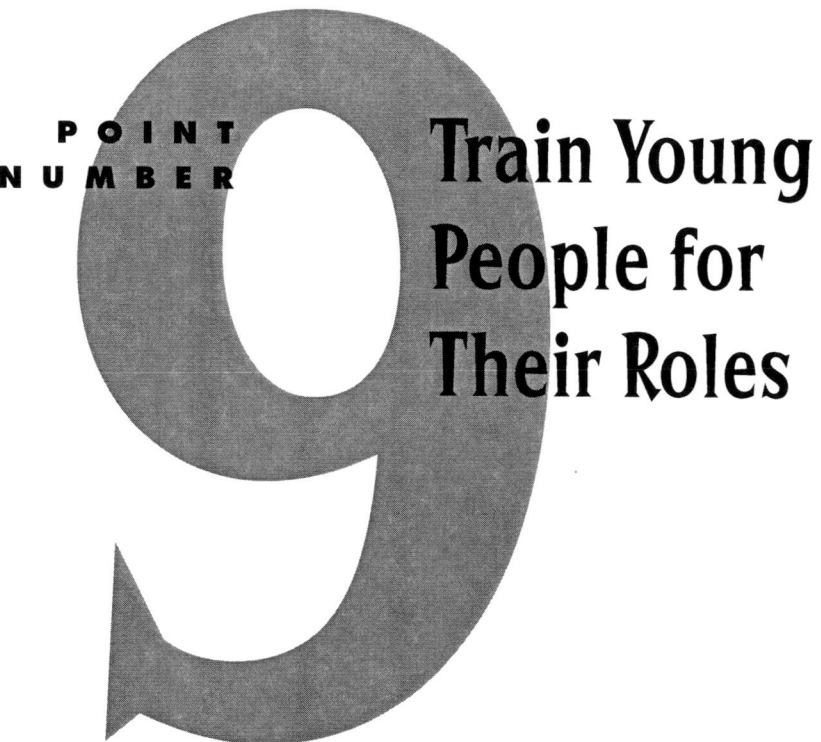

POINT
NUMBER

Train Young People for Their Roles

This chapter offers a step-by-step process for designing training programs and offers possible topics and strategies to include.

1

2

3

4

5

6

7

8

9

10

11

12

13

14

"The best result of being on the board grant committee has been breaking through my shyness and coming out with moderate aggressiveness. I ask questions instead of sitting there pondering them. I loudly voice my own opinions instead of whispering them. I introduce myself to people unknown to me instead of letting someone else do it. And I speak my words without fidgeting. I don't feel like a tiny mouse anymore. I feel more like that great Statue of Liberty."

—Huong Hoang
Honoree at Youth on Board's annual
Strength in Numbers event

What happened to Ms. Hoang didn't happen overnight. Nor did it happen without intention. The chair of the board she was on remembers, "It was no easy task getting her out of her shell. Yes, she was ready to come out, but she needed the assistance of public speaking and debate training, as well as training in other topics. She needed safe environments where she could test being outspoken, being bold, and letting out a very different side of herself."

It is amazing how much young people can develop with a little investment in information and skills training. Your short-term investment in training will pay off in the long term—both for the personal development of the individual and for his/her effectiveness as a member of the board and of the community. Though we focus in this chapter on training young people, these general training plans can be used for everyone.

At Youth on Board, we talk often of three different types of ongoing training programs, which are:

Training for young people: This is training specifically designed for young people in order to develop their skills, confidence, and knowledge. This is the primary focus of this chapter.

Training for all governance members: Training for all members is touched upon in this chapter, but is better addressed by generic board training materials. These can be obtained from the National Center for Nonprofit Boards[1].

Intergenerational training: Intergenerational training is done with both young people and adults to help improve communication and teamwork. We focus exclusively on this in the next chapter. As you read through this chapter and get a sense of the basic process for designing a training plan, you may begin to think about how you might develop a training program for both youth and adults.

Steps for Developing a Training Program for Young People

Putting a new training component in place, or enhancing an existing program, can take as much time and resources as you are willing to put into it. The following five steps, which we describe in detail, will help you create or improve a training program for young people:

1. Select training topics that will help achieve your goals.

2. Choose innovative learning strategies to achieve your goals.

3. Recruit people and prepare materials.

4. Implement the plan.

5. Review and evaluate the process.

[1] See the *Resource Directory*, located at the end of this book, for National Center for Nonprofit Boards contact information.

1. Select training topics that will help you achieve your goals.

What topics does your group care about? In order to develop effective training programs, it is important to define areas where young people will need more information or improved skills. In developing your training goals, remember to include young people in the process. While you may know what you want your young board members to learn, it is equally important to determine what training *they* want.

There are many topics you will want to cover during specific training sessions, from the philosophical (the purpose of the board) to the practical (how to give a presentation). Here are just a few topics and training outlines to consider, taken from Youth on Board's SpringBoard training course:

What's up with nonprofits?

Do you ever wonder how an organization works? Do you have a project you would like to see happen in your neighborhood? Through our 7 Stages for Developing a Nonprofit, you can create your own fantasy nonprofit based on your very own project. Explore what nonprofit really means, the significance of a mission statement, and how organizations get money.

Building your listening skills

Keeping your ears open is a huge challenge—it's so easy to miss the important things that other people are saying. Learn tips and techniques that will help you pay closer attention to people. Learn how, by paying attention to people, you can help them think in new ways.

Identity groups

Participants engage in team-building by breaking into groups with common identities, then reporting back to the group as a whole about discoveries they have made. For example, some identity groups include athletes, Latino men, and Black women. Each identity group would brainstorm about questions like, "What is best about being a member of this group?" "What is hardest about being part of this group?" After brainstorming, the entire group reconvenes to discuss what the different group members have learned, thus allowing everyone to learn about each other.

Facilitating groups and planning an interactive agenda

To keep a group engaged, you'll need an interactive agenda. Learn techniques like speakouts, listening in pairs, and icebreakers, which make meetings not only more fun but also more productive.

The caring leader

Every good leader knows how to listen to and openly appreciate other people. Participants sharpen these skills and recognize their own leadership abilities.

Basic fundraising

Most projects require fundraising and money management. Participants learn about grant writing, developing budgets, planning an event, and asking for donations.

Time management and how to say no

Do you have a lot to do and no idea how to get it all done? Are you being asked to do everything for everyone? Learn how to prioritize and say "yes" to opportunities while saying "no" to what does not fit into your plan.

Supporting leaders and dealing with dissent

As we all know, it is much easier to criticize someone else's leadership than to lead ourselves. Participants consider methods for supporting other leaders and ways to value people who disagree within a group.

Participants should consider methods for supporting other leaders and ways to value people who disagree within a group.

2. Choose innovative learning strategies to achieve your goals.

Unfortunately, when most of us think about training, we get stuck in the classroom mentality—endless lectures and textbooks. But learning can be a lot more interactive and experimental. There are scores of people, places, activities, books, and films that we can learn from. Which ones are right for your group?

Here are just a few strategies that you might think about. After reviewing these, you may want to get together with staff or other group members and brainstorm your own list. Also refer to the tips outlined in *Point 11: Make Meetings Work*.

Community resources

Bring in speakers from community businesses or from organizations similar to your own to conduct workshops on given subjects, such as fundraising, making committees work, public speaking, budgeting, etc.

Book/article groups

Pick a couple of books or articles to read as a group and get together to discuss them. *Nonprofit Boards* is a book (published by the National Center for Nonprofit Boards) you might start with, or choose one that is specific to your organization's mission. If young people don't have much time, pick a chapter, rather than tackle an entire book. It might be best to assign reading during the summer, when students often have more free time.

Spend time on the job

Have the young person come and spend an afternoon in the office—helping out, getting a sense of what goes on in a normal day, and seeing the organization from a different perspective. This may also give them the opportunity to ask questions they might not feel comfortable raising during a meeting.

9

Shadowing

Have the new youth members of your group observe the executive director (or other board member) at a meeting where he/she is giving a presentation. In the future, you might ask youth members to speak on behalf of the organization.

Scavenger hunts

This is a fun way to learn new information and develop teamwork. Create a list and send trainees out to find the information or items on the list. For example, you could plan a scavenger hunt around your office and make a list that includes fundraising files, a staple, a business card from the marketing director, and food from the vending machine. Scavenger hunts allow young people to become familiar with your building and help them feel comfortable there.

Site visits

Schedule a visit to a local city office, nonprofit, or business. Use the trip as an opportunity to expand young people's knowledge about what is in their community and where resources exist. For example, go to a bank for a workshop on investment and the art of philanthropy. Head to the mayor's office for an overview of a recent city plan.

Presentations

Don't underestimate the amount of learning that can happen when someone is under pressure. Setting up a situation where young people can present information or a project is a great way to help them develop both their knowledge base and their presentation skills.

3. Recruit people and prepare materials.

Once your needs are defined, there are many places to find training resources. Here are a couple of places to look:

Youth on Board's training resources

Youth on Board has several training resources for individuals and groups, ranging from two-hour introductory sessions to week-long train-the-trainer courses. For more information, give us a call at 617/623-9900 x1242, or e-mail us at Youthboard@aol.com.

Local and regional resources

Most cities have training that is offered through the United Way, colleges, universities, or the local chapter of the American Society for Training and Development. These resources may be more useful for organizations that function on a broad local or regional level, because it's more likely for these organizations to be training a large number of people at a time.

Training manuals

If you want to design your own program, there are a host of training manuals that you can find in the library, on the Web, or on the shelves of youth-serving organizations in your area. These are a great resource for specific workshop formats and layouts.

Local historic or cultural spaces

There is a lot of learning that can go on at libraries, museums, historic buildings, and historic landmarks. Obtain a list of places in your area from the chamber of commerce or the mayor's office and think creatively. Maybe you can visit the state house to see an exhibit on how legislation gets passed, or attend various exhibits at a museum to understand different cultures.

Local youth organizations

Local youth organizations may know of great trainers you can call on. There may also be a corporate training office or network in your area. Don't hesitate to make cold calls and ask for help. You might be surprised to find how many people are willing to provide training and education for young board members.

9

4. Implement the plan.

As the saying goes, "There is nothing to it, but to do it." Have fun with whatever you choose, and remember to allow yourself to fail. It's equally important to allow your training plan to be implemented in an appropriate time frame. Trying to do everything at once, or, having training sessions too few and far between, decreases your chances of success. It may take a while to learn what works, especially if this process is new to you.

5. Review and evaluate the process.

If you are going to design a training plan that has long-term impact, you've got to set in motion some input, review, and evaluation processes. You can host focus groups once a year about the training that is being implemented, hand out evaluations at the end of each training session, or have an individual review session with each board member every year and discuss training.

Consider doing a pre- and post-test to measure the learning curve of your board members. What do they know after a year on the board that they didn't know before? Try documenting members' progress on video. This is a fun way to help them see themselves and their own development. How did they act at their first board meeting, and then six months later, or after one year?

What's most important is that you create measurement standards that track the growth or learning of trainees. Use these standards to evaluate how well, or poorly, you have done after your training component is implemented.

When the Youth Corps of Noble County Community Foundation[2] in Noble County, IN, needed to learn the basics of being on a board, they turned to Community Partnerships with Youth[3] (CPY), who then conducted their Youth in Governance training. Youth Corps members learned all about trusteeship and what it means to be on a board, as well as how to lead a meeting by using Robert's Rules of Order. After the training, they were so excited about what they had learned that they wanted to offer the skills and experience to youth outside of their organization. They recruited people from 12 community agencies that wanted young people to join their boards of directors and recruited other young people to join them in learning all about boards like they had. CPY conducted additional training at the Youth Corps site.

[2] Noble County Community Foundation, 2092 North State Road 9, Albion, IN 46701. Phone: 219/636-3436.

[3] See the *Resource Directory*, located at the end of this book, for Community Partnerships with Youth contact information.

Create a Training Plan

What is your training plan? Follow the example below to help guide you as you think about a plan for one training objective. The example is written in narrative form so you'll understand the process thoroughly. Use the blank spaces to create your own training plan, which can be in narrative or outline form.

Step 1: Select training topics that will help achieve your goals.

Our goal is to have each young person feel comfortable and able to make a presentation to the full board. Our training topic to help us achieve this goal is public speaking.

Step 2: Choose innovative learning strategies.

We decided the best way to teach young people presentation skills would be to conduct three, two-hour interactive workshops over the course of three weeks. Upon completion of the workshops, each participant will receive a "Certificate of Completion," and be required to make a presentation to the entire board within six months.

Step 3: Recruit people and prepare materials.

We decided that it would be best to hire someone from the community to conduct the workshops. After brainstorming ideas on where to find the best and most affordable people, we discovered that a daughter of one of our board members is in graduate school studying public relations. Another board member called her, and she agreed to conduct the workshops for free to gain training experience.

Step 4: Implement the plan.

The trainer gave us a list of dates and times that she was available. Included on that list was materials that she anticipated needing for her presentations (overhead projector, microphone, podium, etc.). We designated a staff member to reserve the conference room for the workshops, and ensure that her material list was available. The same staff member agreed to attend the workshops to make sure everything went smoothly, and he reported that the workshops were educational, interactive, and entertaining.

Step 5: Review and evaluate the process.

We discovered that we should have consulted with our young board members before scheduling the training workshops. It turns out that some of the other dates our trainer was available would have worked better for our trainees. As it stands, one of our young members did not receive any training, and another was only able to attend one workshop. As to the success of the training itself, the young people who completed the workshops have made presentations to the board. Each board member was asked to evaluate and rate each presentation based on criteria outlined by the trainer and provided to the board before she left. Overall, the trainees did very well. We plan to have them make presentations to the board until they feel comfortable with their new skill.

Based on the example above, create your own plan on the next page:

Step 1: Select training topics that will help achieve your goals.

Step 2: Choose innovative learning strategies.

 Step 3: Recruit people and prepare materials.

Step 4: Implement the plan.

Step 5: Review and evaluate the process.

58 Day Street, P.O. Box 440322, Somerville, MA 02144 • 617.623.9900 x1242

POINT
NUMBER

10

Conduct Intergenerational Training

This chapter discusses the importance of conducting intergenerational training and offers a training module to try out with your group.

Imagine how all the "good old boys" felt back when women were first being integrated into board room settings. Just as many young people are not used to being in adult environments, and there are many adults who have not worked in environments where young people participate as equals.

It is important to recognize that adding youth to your governance structure will be viewed as radical change by some, and that all members will require some degree of acclimation. Training members of your governing structure and staff in the areas of relationship building, communication, and listening skills can be crucial to success.

When we have asked adult participants in Youth on Board's intergenerational workshops what was the most powerful part of the training for them, they have said things like, "It made a huge difference to hear what young people in my group were really thinking," and, "I really forgot what it was like to be young. It was great to be reminded of my youth—both the good and bad parts."

The focus of intergenerational training is to bridge the gap between adults and young people so they can work more effectively together. Though the generation gap may seem unfathomably deep, the truth is that intergenerational training is relatively easy. All adults were young people once, so the trick is to help them remember what is was like growing up. In addition, this training allows young people to speak freely and express their ideas about more than just what may occur at board meetings. Often, intergenerational training exercises leave all participants with a stronger sense of admiration for one another. Trust is easier to build once a solid foundation of respect is laid.

10

A Sample Intergenerational Training Exercise

What follows is a sample portion of the Youth on Board SureShot training exercise that we recommend for all groups that are involving young people in leadership positions. It consists of activities involving both youth and adults, so it should be adapted as it makes sense for your group. This training exercise is designed to be led by one person, and is written for the workshop leader. Time limits should be adjusted according to group size, and breaks should be inserted into the exercise whenever needed. All worksheets and handouts referenced are located, in order, at the end of this chapter.

"An Introduction to Youth in Decision Making" Session Outline

Introduction

- Welcome
- Review session goals

Why youth in decision making?

- Work in pairs
- Review "Why Young People Should Be Decision Makers"

Beyond barriers

- Negative message brainstorm
- Review "Defining Adultism" worksheet

Doing it right

- Review "14 Points for Successfully Involving Youth in Decision Making" handout
- Review "Principles for Young People" worksheet
- Review "Principles for Allies of Young People" worksheet

Next steps

- Development of next steps

Closing

- Discussion of group next steps
- Appreciations

Facilitator's Notes

Introduction

Welcome

1) Review session goals (6 minutes):

The goals of this intergenerational training exercise are:

• To have adults see themselves as allies for youth and advocates for greater youth involvement in every way.

• To have young people learn how to advocate for themselves, working with both adults and other young people.

• To have staff and board members recognize the structures and attitudes within their organization that may deter youth involvement.

• To have staff and board members assess their organizations' readiness and commitment to involving youth in decision making.

• To have everyone recognize the value of young people in the governance of organizations.

• To have everyone develop specific personal and organizational next steps regarding youth in decision making.

Why youth in decision making?

This section answers the basic question, Why youth in decision making? To some it may seem perfectly apparent, but others may have trouble articulating the reasons why. Still others may not really be sure why youth need to be in decision-making positions at all. The following two activities will help the group explore their excitement and anxiety about young people as decision makers.

2) Work in pairs (15 minutes):

Ask the group to break into pairs. Encourage people to partner with others they don't know well. Each person take up to three minutes to answer the following questions. After both people have taken a turn, then the pairs can discuss their answers.

Imagine that your organization is being half-run by young people. Half of the board consists of young people, as does half of the staff. What is exciting about this scenario? What is challenging? (Be honest. Regardless of age, we all have something that scares us about involving youth.)

After the pairs discuss these questions, ask three or four volunteers to quickly report back to the whole group on their responses. If people do not respond, pose one of the following questions: What kind of responses did different people have to this scenario? Did any two people in a pair find themselves with strikingly different responses? Was anyone surprised by his or her own response?

3) Review the "Why Young People Should Be Decision Makers" handout (10 minutes):

Pass out copies of the "Why Young People Should Be Decision Makers" handout. Explain that these are some of the positive aspects that youth-inclusive groups have discovered about youth involvement. Review the handout with the group, allowing for discussion of each point. Also ask the group to share additional ideas they may have regarding the positive aspects of involving youth in decision making.

Beyond barriers

At some point in our lives, we've all experienced unfair treatment because of our age. It is important for everyone to remember the negative ways youth are sometimes treated. Ask the group if they've ever heard the term "adultism." Explain that every person

Every concerned parent, teacher, or youth worker knows the kinds of stereotypes that exist about youth and how those stereotypes can work against individuals.

who tries to make the world better for young people is working against adultism. Every concerned parent, teacher, or youth worker knows the kinds of stereotypes that exist about youth and how those stereotypes can work against individuals, as demonstrated in Step 4 below. Those stereotypes are adultist, just like the stereotypes that exist about African Americans or Asians are racist. Acknowledge that everyone in the room is there because they believe that youth should be more involved and less marginalized.

During these activities, and for the remainder of the workshop, the following tips may help you be sensitive to "hot button" issues:

- Acknowledge the difficult job parents have. Most parents do a great job, especially considering the balancing act they must perform; it's incredibly difficult to watch out for young people and yet let them learn from their own experiences.

- Youth workers and teachers experience a similar conflict. Recognize their dual duties of advocating for youth while simultaneously fulfilling their roles as teachers and mentors.

- Remember that it's fine for people to disagree with the concept of adultism. That they think about the concept and consider the idea is a positive step.

Lastly, remember that these next two and other steps should involve light-hearted discussion. Encourage adults in the group to tell stories about their teen years. Change basically comes through self-awareness.

4) Negative messages brainstorm (10 minutes):

Have the group brainstorm negative messages about young people that they have heard or hear. Examples include, "You'll understand when you're older," "Do as I say, not as I do," "Children are best seen and not heard."

5) Review the "Defining Adultism" worksheet, and discuss adultism (15 minutes):

Pass out copies of the "Defining Adultism" worksheet. Ask everyone to turn to the worksheet and gather in pairs. Ask the pairs to develop definitions for adultism, using the worksheet. Give the pairs up to seven minutes to work. Then ask three or four pairs to read their definitions to the group. Finally, ask all pairs to post their definitions along a wall in the room.

Doing it right

Now that we've gotten beyond barriers that get in the way of adults and young people working together, we have to figure out how to build strong youth/adult partnerships and how to do it right.

6) Review "14 Points for Successfully Involving Youth in Decision Making" handout (10 minutes):

Distribute copies of the handout, "14 Points for Successfully Involving Youth in Decision Making." Quickly review these guidelines with the group. In small groups of three to five people, ask everyone to discuss how these guidelines can be followed in your organization. Have each small group share their suggestions for how to implement to the guidelines.

7) Review of "Principles for Young People" worksheet (10 minutes):

Distribute copies of the "Principles for Young People" worksheet to the young people in your group. Ask them to pair up and review the worksheet. Young people should describe to their partner times when they have experienced the principles outlined on the worksheets. Explain that this helps young people recognize what they have already accomplished. At the end of this exercise, invite them to share their stories and discuss the principles with the entire group.

8) Review of "Principles for Allies to Young People" worksheet (10 minutes):

Distribute to the adults in the group copies of the "Principles for Allies to Young People" worksheet, found at the end of *Point 14: Support Young Leaders and Adult Allies*. While the young people are reviewing their worksheet, have the adults pair up and review this one. The directions are the same as those outlined in the previous activity.

Next steps

After this final section, everyone will have the tools and knowledge to begin working for greater youth involvement.

8) Development of next steps (15 minutes):

Pass out copies of the "Youth Governing Our Communities" worksheet. Ask everyone to gather into small groups of three to five people. Each group should fill out the worksheet together. As part of this exercise, each person should say one thing they have learned during the entire workshop. Remind everyone that their personal or organizational next step can be almost anything, as long as it leads to a deepened involvement of youth in governance. After the small groups have completed the worksheet, the next steps should then be reported to the entire group.

Closing

9) Highlights, appreciations, and follow-up (10 minutes):

Discuss any next steps the group might take as a whole. Finally, ask each person to name a highlight from the meeting and an appreciation of the whole group and/or the people within it. This concludes the "An Introduction to Youth in Decision Making" intergenerational training exercise.

Reminders for facilitators

Before undertaking this exercise, there are a few things the facilitator should keep in mind:

Laughter is a magic tool. Don't underestimate how important it can be for people to laugh together. Laughter helps people feel comfortable with one another. Adults can be a bit tight-lipped when discussing some of the topics included in this training exercise. Laughing allows them the freedom to let go of their inhibitions for a little while. This exercise should leave people feeling uplifted and inspired.

Respect where adults are coming from. It is important to first appreciate where adults are coming from before suggesting alternative ways of approaching problems. The feelings of adult allies tend to fall into two categories: some feel as if they are doing enough for youth, others feel as if they are *not* doing enough. During this training, keep in mind that some adults may interpret statements made by young people as being negative toward them, and other adults may feel guilty because they wish young people had no complaints. Continue to remind adults throughout the training that, no matter how they may be feeling, they are wonderful individuals and they are doing a great job supporting young people.

The most important thing that can happen during this training is that people really listen to each other. Don't worry as much about getting through the agenda as creating space for participants to open up and hear what each other is saying.

Know that important things are happening. Even when you can't see it, people are learning. Though it's hard to measure, trust that all of you are growing from this experience.

The five C's of the good facilitator

Clarity: You have to know your stuff and know how to communicate your message clearly. Before every workshop, allow plenty of time for preparation and review your curriculum thoroughly. Always be on the look out for materials, contacts, and experiences that can enhance your insights into youth action.

Connection: To really lead a group you have to connect with them. Make a concerted effort to talk to people individually, remember their names, and try to understand their needs.

Caring: If you care about and respect a group, you will find the connection you need. All the training and curricula on earth can't compete with the expertise you gain simply by caring about and respecting your participants.

Changeable: You've read the curriculum, assembled perfect participant packets, and even drawn a big, welcoming smiley-face on the board before class. Now, just toss it all out the window! No matter how much preparation you've done, you must be ready for serious improvisation if the workshop or class is not working for your participants. This can be as simple as leading an unscheduled game to pep up your group or as complex as overhauling the focus of an entire class. This material is a tool to supplement your own knowledge and skills. Veering away from it will occasionally be necessary.

Confidence: "Our deepest fear is not that we are inadequate. Our deepest fear is that we are powerful beyond measure. ... And as we let our own light shine, we unconsciously give other people

10

permission to do the same." Nelson Mandela said that. So be bold, take the lead, do your best, and shine on!

Additional Intergenerational Training Topics

There are a host of other intergenerational trainings that you can conduct with your group. In this publication alone, you have many worksheets that can be used in an intergenerational training setting. If you do conduct additional training of this type, consider the following topics:

Speak out on early years. Invite young people to speak for five minutes each about what it is like to be 14 years old, or 12, or 18. Immediately following the presentations, have adults pair up and talk about what they remember about being that age.

Celebrate allies to young people. Spend an evening celebrating what adults are doing to support young people. This can be an event complete with refreshments, party favors, and games, if you like. The work of committed adults rarely receives much recognition (at least in the short term). A celebration gives everyone a chance to appreciate others, and themselves. As part of the event, have each adult answer the question, "What have you done lately to support young people and their development?"

◆ As part of an intergenerational training exercise conducted at a leadership conference in Alexandria, South Africa, young people got a chance to speak out about what it is like to be young—what obstacles they faced, what about adults made them uncomfortable, what about being young made life fun. Once the students shared their feelings, the adult participants started, one by one, to share stories about their younger years—when they rebelled and why, and what they missed about being that age. Everyone ended up smiling and laughing, and finding out that they had more in common than they ever thought. Both sides left the training with new insight, and adults gained a greater appreciation for the intelligence of the young people at the conference.

◆ A high school principal in Marquette, MI, would not allow public displays of affection at his school's dances. Young people were furious about this policy, but could not figure out an appropriate way to vent their anger and frustration. During a Youth on Board intergenerational training conducted at the school, young people got a chance to talk openly about how this policy impacted their sense of rights and the way they wanted to express their feelings. The principal confessed that he was unaware that young people felt so passionately about the policy, and he acknowledged the validity of their opinions. Soon after the intergenerational training, the school dance policy was changed.

10

Why Young People Should Be Decision Makers[1]

It's a diversity issue.

Even though they may not have years of formal experience, youth offer intelligence, creative thinking, and a valuable outlook on the world that is seldom introduced into the governance of organizations. While age diversity might not show up on a typical diversity chart, it is a critical element for boards that want to embrace many voices and perspectives.

But it is important to remember that there is no "stock" young person. Their opinions and ideas are as varied as any other group's. Age is only one shaping force in their lives. Like the rest of us, young people's outlooks are deeply affected by their personal experiences—their racial, economic, religious, and sexual identities, and their individual personalities.

It's a democracy issue.

To make a democracy work, all people need to be heard. This includes the voices of young people. We need to hear their views, ideas, and passions. We also need to act on their ideas, so that democracy continues to thrive in future generations.

It's a bottom-line issue.

Quite simply, young people are uniquely qualified to say what works for young people. By relying on young decision makers to provide personal insights, talk with friends, and organize youth focus groups, organizations can save time and money by catching decisions that might not work well with young people *before* they are enacted and fail.

It's a civil rights issue.

Nowhere in the U.S. Declaration of Independence is there a stipulation concerning age. "*All* men are created equal." *All* are entitled to "certain unalienable rights." So why is it that in this country decisions that affect a significant segment of the population are made by others? In far too many situations, young people are not being heard. Their rights are being disregarded or violated, and adults do not seem to hear or care about it. This needs to change. A shift is needed in our communities to allow young people's concerns to be heard and taken seriously. They have the same right as adults to voice their fears, hopes, and ideas.

It's a youth development issue.

Being a leader can change the life of a young person. Leadership helps young people develop confidence in their opinions and their ideas. For many young people, this will be the first time their ideas have been instrumental in real decision making. In addition to fostering confidence, participating as a leader can introduce youth to a range of other skills—public speaking, budgeting,

58 Day Street, P.O. Box 440322, Somerville, MA 02144 • 617.623.9900 x1242

leading projects and committees, and networking, to name a few.

By creating visible youth decision-making positions, you can impact the self- esteem of young people in your organization and throughout your community. It bolsters *all* young people's self-confidence to see their peers being taken seriously, and having youth positions will generate a positive reputation for your organization or initiative.

It's a long-term growth issue.

Youth can provide a new generation of leadership. Some organizations have looked around and noticed that everyone on staff and in decision-making positions is getting older. Adding young people to the governance of an aging organization can usher in a new generation of leadership.

It's an organizational culture issue.

Youth can enliven the atmosphere of your organization. Young people bring energy and enthusiasm to their work. They often remind us that work and fun are not mutually exclusive. In addition, most organizations incorporate more interactive work processes when they involve youth. Techniques like small group discussions or brainstorming encourage teamwork and foster better communication by giving people a chance to be heard. Everyone, regardless of age, is at their best and brightest when they are comfortable expressing themselves.

It's a community outreach issue.

Young people bring an entirely new community of contacts to your organization. If young people are out front and vocal about your committee or organization, other young people will be drawn to find out about what you are doing. They are able to plug into the world of their peers in ways that adults, as outsiders, simply cannot. Keep in mind that word-of-mouth advertising is *extremely* effective among young people. By adding youth to your decision-making body, you are expanding your circle of clients, constituents, or consumers, and adding to their understanding of your group.

It's an integrity issue.

It is important for any organization to involve its constituents. Just as it would not make sense for the NAACP (National Association for the Advancement of Colored People) to be run exclusively by Caucasians, it does not make sense for youth-serving organizations to be run exclusively by adults.

---

[1] Some of the ideas in this text were taken from a speech given by Amy Weisenbach of the National 4-H Council at the 1998 National Assembly Forum.

Defining Adultism

Consider these examples of adultism, created by young people involved in governance structures. In pairs, read the following examples, and then, in each case, answer the following questions: What do the examples have in common? What motivates adults to act this way? After discussing these examples in pairs, reconvene as a group and share your thoughts. To conclude the exercise, each group member should write their own definition for the word "adultism" in the space at the end of this worksheet.

Example 1: Writing "Tasha, age 17," rather than "Tasha Martin." While it's great to demonstrate that young people are involved, you should be very careful not to be condescending. Adults would never write "Jim, age 54" in a professional setting.

Example 2: Considering only age, not experience. Young people's experiences are extremely valuable, even if they are not traditional professional experiences.

Example 3: Asking young people, "Do you understand?" in a condescending way. It's great to be thoughtful when someone looks lost, whether they are an adult or a young person, but be careful not to put young people on the spot.

Example 4: Assuming young people won't be able to understand a topic or concept rather than taking the time to explain it to them.

Example 5: Making condescending comments like, "You're still a little wet behind the ears!" "When you grow up you'll understand." "It's just a phase; you'll grow out of it."

Example 6: Asking young people to handle only small or menial tasks. As with adults, simple tasks need to be balanced with important and challenging projects in order for work to be exciting and fulfilling.

Example 7: Being surprised when young people say something intelligent, when they are dressed appropriately, or when they are well organized. Comments such as, "You're so smart! I can't believe you're only 15!"

Example 8: Assuming that young people only know about issues concerning youth.

Example 9: Ignoring young people when you are busy with "more important" things.

Example 10: Using jargon that is unfamiliar to young people. Help young people learn the language used in your field. In the meantime, remember to phrase things so everyone can understand.

Your definition of adultism:

_____

_____

_____

_____

14 Points:
Successfully Involving Youth in Decision Making

Point 1: Know Why You Want to Involve Young People

• **It's a civil rights issue:** Nowhere in the U. S. Declaration of Independence is there a stipulation concerning age. *"All* men are created equal." *All* are entitled to "certain unalienable rights." So why is it that in this country decisions that affect a significant segment of the populations are made by others? In far too many situations, young people are not being heard. Their rights are being disregarded or violated, and adults do not seem to hear or care about it. This needs to change. A shift is needed in our communities to allow young people's concerns to be heard and taken seriously. They have the same right as adults to voice their hopes, ideas, and fears.

• **It's a long-term growth issue:** Educating youth about the ideals of the nonprofit sector and community service can plant the seeds of social responsibility in their heads. Similarly, youth can provide a new generation of leadership. Some organizations have looked around and noticed that everyone on staff and in decision-making positions is getting older. Adding young people to the governance of an aging organization can usher in a new generation of leadership.

• **Develop clear goals and objectives:** It is important for everyone in your organization to determine the exact reasons why you want to involve young people in decision-making roles. Defining objectives is a way to create a benchmark for your group. While larger goals will keep you focused in the right direction, your objectives will lead the way. Objectives should be specific, tangible, and attainable.

Point 2: Conduct an Organizational Assessment

• **Assess your readiness:** The purpose of conducting an organizational assessment is to determine what is needed in order for youth to be successfully integrated into your governance structure. Are you already strong in most areas related to supporting youth involvement, or do you have specific areas for major growth?

• **Investing your board and staff:** Assembling a board committee to research and help prepare for youth involvement can be an excellent way to invest your board in this idea. You can also include individual conversations with all board members to make sure they understand and support youth involvement. Your staff can be the cornerstone that makes this project stand. In many organizations, staff members support new young members by helping them prepare for meetings or by providing transportation. This kind of undertaking can be a great way to foster a deeper relationship among your staff, board, and young people.

• **Investing young people:** Recruiting for new youth members is a great chance to educate the youth in your program about the role of your governing body. It is important that the young people with whom you work understand what the group does and know that young people play and integral role.

Point 3: Determine Your Model for Youth Involvement

• **Two general approaches:** All of the approaches to youth involvement fall into two general categories: 1) **Involve young people directly in an existing adult governing body:** for example, add several youth positions to an existing board, church council, community task force, city commission, or advisory board; or 2) **Create an all-youth or youth-run adjunct body.**

Point 4: Identify Organizational Barriers

• **Institutionalize youth in governance:** Organizations need to move past youth in governance as a good idea and build it into their structure. Most governance bodies involving youth have written into their bylaws that a certain number of members must be young people. If you are creating a youth advisory group, ensure that it is a permanent structure, not one that will disappear with a change in administration.

• **Conflict of interest:** Many organizations recruit among youth currently involved with their programs. It can be a real asset to both the governing body and a youth member if she or he is already familiar with the program. You may, however, encounter concerns about conflict of interest. Your group should establish clear conflict of interest guidelines and apply these to any potential new youth or adult members.

• **Budget and staff considerations:** The idea of involving youth may appeal to your organization, but there are budget concerns to address. Do you have the staff time, transportation funds, and the petty cash for such things as reimbursements and refreshments at evening meetings?

Point 5: Overcome Attitudinal Barriers

• **Adults must overcome their own stereotypes:** We all have stereotypes about young people. To work well with young people, we must recognize these negative assumptions and learn to share real authority.

• **Youth need to know that they deserve to have a say:** Young people deserve to have their voices heard. Recognizing this isn't always easy because we are so often told that young people have nothing to say. Youth need to recognize their own value.

• **Speak a common language:** Most professional settings speak a very "adult" language, using jargon, abbreviations, and references to organizations only commonly known to adults. When young people are involved, ideas must be presented in a way that allows everyone to understand.

Point 6: Address Legal Issues

• **The obligations of board members:** Above all, the directors of a nonprofit corporation are bound by two general types of legal duties: A **duty of care**—the duty to perform their responsibilities in good faith and in a manner that they reasonably believe to be in the best interests of the corporation, and with such care as an ordinary person in a like position in a similar corporation would use in similar circumstances; and a **duty of loyalty**—the duty to keep the interest of the corporation paramount above personal interests when acting for or on behalf of the corporation.

• **Legality of young people serving on boards:** Because each state makes its own laws, you should check to see what the laws are around youth governance in your state. For the most part, you will find three different kinds of state rulings: 1) A law that

58 Day Street, P.O. Box 440322, Somerville, MA 02144 • 617.623.9900 x1242

says it is legal for youth to serve as directors with age constraints; 2) A law stating that it is not legal for young people to vote on boards if they are under a certain age; and 3) No law on the issue at all.

• **Contract considerations:** Though many boards do not often enter into legal contracts, it is important to note that age-specific contract laws do exist. Your board should research the contract laws in your state.

Point 7: Recruit Young People

• **Be clear about what you want:** As with any strong team, a governing body should reflect an even balance of interest, skills, and diversity among its members. There are some characteristics that are important for every member of your governing body to possess and some skills that only a few members need to have. Before selecting new members, consider creating a governing body profile—a simple list of characteristics already found in the group, as well as those skills you hope new members will possess.

• **Choose motivated and committed youth:** You will want to choose a youth member just as you would any other governance body member. Consider individual strengths. Be sure the person you select has the commitment, motivation, and time to make his or her involvement work. Never select a young person just because you think it would be a good experience for her or him.

• **Add two or more young people:** Adding more than one young person to an adult governing body offers more support to youth in governance positions. It is important that young people not feel alone or isolated in your group.

Point 8: Create a Strong Orientation Process

• **New member orientation:** Your orientation program for new members should clearly outline the basics of your organization's mission, programs, structure, and history, as well as a forthright description of the relationships among your staff, board, and funders. You should also review the roles and responsibilities of your governing body.

• **Letter of agreement:** All members should receive a detailed letter of agreement that describes their term and responsibilities. This agreement clarifies expectations for all parties and solidifies commitment.

• **Parental orientation:** In addition to conducting an in-depth orientation with young people, it is important to help their parents or guardians feel comfortable with your organization as well. Parents play an important role in the success of your young board members. Parents or guardians should know at least one individual from your group.

Point 9: Train Young People for Their Roles

• **Training for young people:** Young people will need skills training that covers reading budgets, working on committees, and other bits of governance-related knowledge. Many groups go as far as setting up a buddy system, pairing a seasoned member with each new member to handle questions, advice, and general support.

• **Training for adults:** Most adults have never carefully considered the assumptions they hold about young people. Before bringing youth into the governance of your organization, your governance environment should be inviting to them. For your adult members, this means exploring their own stereotypes about youth and learning to be good allies for young people.

• **Be innovative:** Unfortunately, when most of us think about training, we get stuck in the classroom mentality—endless lectures and textbooks. But learning can be a lot more interactive and experimental. There are scores of people, places, activities, books, and films that we can learn from. Which ones are right for your group?

Point 10: Conduct Intergenerational Training

• **Intergenerational training:** Once young people are in decision-making positions, you will need to continue training the whole group. This is a wonderful way to foster interpersonal relationships among your members and further diminish any tensions that may exist because of age. The focus of intergenerational training is to bridge the gap between adults and young people so they can work more effectively together.

• **Keep it fun:** Don't underestimate how important it can be for people to laugh together. Adults can be a bit tight-lipped when discussing some of the topics that should be included in intergenerational training (such as how youth *really* view adults, and vise versa). Laughing allows everyone the freedom to let go of his or her inhibitions for a little while.

• **Listening is key:** The most important thing that can happen during this training is that people really listen to each other. Don't worry as much about getting through an agenda as creating space for participants to open up and hear what each other is saying.

Point 11: Make Meetings Work

• **Meeting times:** Your meeting times may conflict with young people's schedules. While young people may not have teleconferences to keep them from meetings, they do have basketball games, school play rehearsals, and family engagements. They, in fact, have less control over their time than most adults do.

• **Interactive agendas:** Everyone appreciates an engaging meeting. A few small changes to your meeting structure can help everyone be involved, especially young people. Include small group time where everyone has a chance to speak. Go around the group and ask each person to give feedback. When reviewing a budget, do it in pairs, and always make sure there is plenty of opportunity to ask questions.

• **Use appreciations:** How often does it happen that you are plugging away at work, not getting much done, and maybe even feeling a little hopeless about how much more you have to do? Then someone walks by and says, "Hey! You're doing a really good job. Thanks!" You return to your work, but the load feels a little lighter. This is the power of appreciation. We suggest that you create a regular structured time for appreciations during meetings, because many work settings are just not in the habit of doing this kind of thing.

Point 12: Develop a Mentoring Plan

• **Recommended for new members:** When joining a group, new members of all ages can use the advice of a buddy who already knows the ropes. Young people are unique because they seldom have prior professional experience. Mentors, whether they be experienced adult or youth group members, provide critical support to young people by helping them learn new terms, understand organizational culture, and build confidence to act as full partners in the group.

• **Know your responsibilities:** In order for mentoring to work, mentors should know what's expected of them. There are a range of responsibilities that a good mentor should have, but most importantly, mentors should make sure that new members attend meetings, have the support they need, and are well-oriented to the organization they have joined.

• **Tips for new young members:** Young people should remember that their mentors are there to help them. In order for this relationship to run smoothly, young people should, among other things: trust their mentor; ask lots of questions; and speak up when they have an opinion.

Point 13: Build Youth/Adult Relationships

• **Relationships are of primary importance:** Strong relationships are key to all successful programs and social change movements. From local community efforts to international movements, it is a solid network of committed people that creates social change. This human caring is where deep, permanent transformation comes from.

• **Adults, go easy on yourselves:** Adults tend to have a bad habit of being hard on themselves. They often feel they don't do enough, or that they should have it all figured out by now. Blaming yourself or other adults is never an effective path to change. We need to recognize that anything we understand about working with young people is wonderful.

• **Remember the importance of involving parents:** It is vital to include parents right from the start. Get to know them. Share information with them. Answer their questions. Invite them to events. Appreciate them and the work that their child is doing for your group. Convey to them your enthusiasm for the work you're doing. In addition, let young people know that you are going to be talking to their parents. Let them know that you are not checking up on them or breaking any confidentiality, but that talking with their parents will insure that they know how important young people are to your organization.

Point 14: Create Support Networks

• **Network young leaders:** As adults work to forge strong relationships with young people, they must be mindful of the relationships that youth build with each other. Young people on boards of directors, city councils, or in other leadership positions can be excellent support for one another. By being networked with other youth leaders, young people see that they are not alone in their work and that other youth care about the same issues.

• **Adults, support each other:** It is not easy to remember that you need support too. As adults working with youth, we tend to put our own personal growth and ourselves on the back burner. Just as youth need the support of other youth, allies to young people need opportunities to talk with one another about their experiences.

Principles for Young People

Items on this list might remind you of you at your best. Think of all the great stuff you've done for those in your age group and briefly describe instances when you have followed several of the principles listed below.

Don't believe negative messages. There are lots of negative messages about young people: "Kids should be seen and not heard." "This hurts me more than it hurts you." "You'll understand when you are older." Many young people hear these messages at home, at school, and on TV. Don't believe them. Simply because you're young does not mean that your ideas are any less important. Even if you think you don't have anything to say, look a little deeper. You know a lot, and you have huge contributions to make.

_____

_____

_____

_____

Remember that you *should* have a say. In fact, your opinion is more than important. It is essential. Even if every-one else doesn't realize it, you have to remember it. Regardless of the negative messages you hear, you and other young people have the power to change your communities and your world. To do so, you must remember it is your right to have a say.

_____

_____

_____

_____

Speak up. Find ways to make your voice heard. You can serve on a board, work with a local youth program, volun-teer, organize a community event, or just talk to your friends about issues that concern you. It's all about being active, taking a stand, and making a difference.

_____

_____

_____

_____

Find friends to support you. Taking action is seldom easy, and it can be even harder if you try and do it alone. Find friends to support you and a team to work with you. Alone you might make a splash, but as a team you can unleash a tidal wave.

_____

_____

_____

_____

Work with your adult allies. There are a lot of adults who do believe that young people should have a say. They often have influence, contacts, and resources that can work in your favor. Don't give up your own judgment, but at the same time remain open to your allies' advise. Their experiences are valuable to you.

_____

_____

_____

_____

Do it again and again. Not everyone is going to hear your message the first time. Whether you are lobbying your school board to include young people or organizing a neighborhood festival, remember to speak your mind over and over again. Don't get discouraged. Believe in your ideas and be persistent.

_____

_____

_____

_____

Youth Governing Our Communities

The following questions are meant for small group discussion. One group member should be chosen to record the group's answers to each question.

1) Whether you or someone else makes it happen, what do you wish would be done for youth in your organization, school, or community?

_____

_____

_____

2) If you had all the time in the world and nobody standing in your way, what would still be your biggest challenge when working with (other) young people?

_____

_____

_____

3) What issues with young people do you personally need to overcome?

_____

_____

_____

4) What are your next steps?

a. _____

_____

b. _____

_____

c. _____

_____

POINT NUMBER

11

Make Meetings Work

This chapter offers innovative strategies for making meetings more exciting and effective. It includes a worksheet to use when planning future meeting agendas.

1
2
3
4
5
6
7
8
9
10
11
12
13
14

*I*magine that you are 16 years old. You're a writer for your high school paper. The big weekly newspaper in your town just selected you as the youth representative on their Community Advisory Committee. What an honor! They really want to hear what you as a young person have to say.

So you're at your first committee meeting. The senior editor opens the meeting with general announcements. You're feeling butterflies. She's probably going to introduce you soon. First item of business—there will be no coffee or doughnuts at this meeting because revenue for the quarter has dropped 30 percent. She explains the impact the revenue loss will have on the newspaper at every level. Thirty minutes later she invites one committee member, an accountant, to give his assessment of the situation. He spends 10 minutes describing in detail the bleakness of the situation and its impact on the newspaper's sponsorship of local community activities. This is followed by a columnist's presentation of his 6,000-word article on the town's new Gum-Free Sidewalk Initiative. Finally, the meeting is adjourned.

No mention of you. No introductions to other committee members, and certainly no input from most of the group on the crisis facing the paper. Obviously the newspaper is missing a valuable resource by not getting feedback from every Community Advisory Committee member. Even though you don't have a lot of financial knowledge, you could have told them about how your school paper recently countered a slump in readership by sponsoring a reader's contest, or you could have contributed to a general discussion on alternative ways to support community activities.

Though this scenario is somewhat exaggerated, it makes the point that, too often, valuable contributions to a meeting are not made because the agenda is not structured well. There is pressure to cover everything within an amount of time that is likely inadequate. Everyone in a group has important contributions to make and deserves a chance to be heard. Without an active role, people simply will not stay committed to an organization or project. Often, though, we don't take steps to insure involvement. Traditional models for professional meetings, chock full of formal reports and lengthy presentations, do not allow for much interaction. Young people and adults who are uncomfortable with this structure or don't feel that their role is important will probably not make solid contributions in such a rigid setting. Every board member wants to leave a meeting feeling like they contributed something.

Many people ask, "How do we fit in more group activities when our meetings are already bursting at the seams?" Part of the challenge is finding creative ways to fold interactive techniques into the topics you already need to discuss. For example, instead of presenting a report on the budget, consider reviewing the budget in small groups.

Remember that a central goal of any council, board, task force, or other group should be to build an active, committed team. Using the following interactive strategies and tools won't require much extra time, yet will deepen members' personal investment in your group. The more invested members feel, the more likely they will be to work hard and remain involved.

A central goal of any council, board, task force, or other group should be to build an active, committed team.

Tips for Making Meetings More Interactive

When integrating any of the following tips into your meeting agenda, be sure to set time limits. Many people complain that making meetings interactive means that meetings have to be that much longer. Not true. Time limits, when set for all agenda items, ensure that meetings don't run any longer than they have to.

Getting off to a good start: Check-ins

It's good to start each meeting with a brief check-in. We often call this a "New and Good," with each person sharing a few sentences about one thing that is new and good in his or her life. Or, you can have each person answer a specific question. If you're organizing a conference, for example, you can go around the table and have each person describe the best or worst conference she or he ever attended.

Why check-in? We've all walked into meetings still focused on the vehicle that cut us off as we were racing to the meeting. Check-ins center us on the task at hand and allow us to share something personal. They are also great ice-breakers. If everyone is given a chance to speak at the beginning of a meeting, they are more likely to feel comfortable speaking out during the rest of the meeting. By fostering personal interest in one another's lives, a stronger team is built.

Talking in pairs

At some point during the meeting, break the group into pairs. Either let people pair off on their own, or put people together in a strategic way. Then pose a question. It might be something that helps the two people get to know one another, such as, "What do you hope to learn while working in this group?" or "What was your favorite time of life?" Or you could ask pairs to solve a specific problem together, such as, "Can you find items that might be cut in this year's budget?" or "What kind of fundraising event would have the most appeal in our town?"

Each person should have enough time to answer the question you pose. Be strict about time limits so both people in each pair have a chance to answer. It might feel awkward to cut people off at first, and you should be sensitive as you do it, but sticking to uniform time limits will keep activities fair for everyone. While one person speaks, the other person can ask questions to help his or her partner along. They should not, however, talk about their own positions, ideas, or stories. The goal is to listen without interrupting.

After pairs have spent a few minutes discussing an issue, they can report the important points of their discussion back to the entire group. There are a number of formats from which to choose: reports can be written, a few groups can give short reports as a sampling, or all groups can report just their main points. Verbal reports from pairings and small groups are not always necessary, and it's important not to let reports go on too long. They can grow dull, and they can also eat into your meeting time.

Why pairs? Pairing is powerful because it gives people a chance to process their ideas in a more comfortable setting before they are asked to speak in front of a group. The feedback people give in pairs also tends to be more direct and more thoughtful. Then, when people are asked for responses in a big group, their ideas will be more thought out. One-on-one listening builds confidence, gets new ideas on the table, and creates a strong team.

Small groups

Small groups can be used like pairs. They require a bit more time, but are very helpful when a group is thinking about a given topic. Small group topics should generally be about problem-solving or planning (e.g., boosting registration for an upcoming conference, or planning youth-led tours of your neighborhood). Different groups can address different topics so several issues can be worked out at the same time.

Small groups can be conducted as formal "go-arounds," during which, like in pairings, each person is allotted a certain amount of time to talk. Or they can be less structured small group discussions, during which everyone is given a chance to speak.

Why small groups? Small groups generate solid ideas that have been refined by the contributions of a number of people. Small group members are more likely to be actively engaged in the thinking process than they would be with a full-sized group.

Brainstorming

Brainstorming is all about unclogging our thought processes and not censoring our ideas because we think they might be wrong. At a meeting, start off by explaining the brainstorm process to your group and then write, where everyone can see, the three guidelines listed below. Name a topic about which you want people to think freely (e.g., topics for upcoming newsletter articles or slogans for a new advertising campaign). Then open the floor to ideas and write each one on a flip chart, adhering to these guidelines:

1) No discussion   2) No criticism   3) Repetition is okay

There should be *no discussions* and *no criticism* of any of the ideas. Interruptions stop the flow of ideas. People should be comfortable tossing out whatever comes to mind. This exercise is meant to generate lots of ideas that may or may not be used. Also remember that *it is fine if ideas are repeated*. Write up each and every one.

Once the allotted time for brainstorming is up, the group can being processing the ideas that are generated. As tempting as it may be to start refining ideas during the brainstorm, get them all out first and save the processing for later.

Why brainstorming? Brainstorms are a safe way for people to contribute their ideas and speak to the group. Brainstorming creates an environment in which people will not be afraid of being judged or criticized. Brainstorms also let people work creatively together. (There is a "Tips for Brainstorming" handout at the end of this chapter.)

Go-around at closing

At the end of the meeting, conduct another brief go-around to wrap things up. The go-around should be something positive—a highlight or an appreciation.

When doing highlights, each person simply tells the group about the part of the meeting that meant the most to him or her. It could be a funny or an insightful moment.

An appreciation is simply naming something you appreciate about someone in the group. For example, "I really think Jon did an excellent job leading our small group through a very tough brainstorm." People may be shy about appreciations at first, but if you persist, they can be very powerful. For more information about appreciations, see the handout at the end of this chapter.

Why go-around? This will help people leave a meeting with a sense of affirmation and a feeling that good things were accomplished through their participation. It also gives everyone a chance to speak. Like other interactive techniques, it is an excellent team builder.

Brainstorming creates an environment in which people will not be afraid of being judged or criticized.

Committee meetings

If you are working with a group that has committees, it is best to break into committees for the last half hour of the general meeting.

Why committee meetings? This gives people a chance to work in these important smaller groups without the hassle of making other arrangements to meet.

How to Prepare an Interactive Agenda

As you sit down to plan a meeting, take a few minutes to ask yourself or your planning group the following questions. Use the worksheet at the end of this chapter to answer them:

- What are our goals for this meeting?

- Which issues require member feedback?

- How can we strategically use the resources of this group?

- How can we let members know that their contributions count?

- How can we structure meetings so everyone is involved?

- Where in the agenda should we incorporate interactive activities?

- What is the goal of the interactive activities: team building, problem solving, or both?

On the following page is a **sample meeting agenda** to use as a reference when planning your own meetings. When making your own agenda, remember to set time limits in accordance with how many people will be attending the meeting.

11

Meeting topic: Planning a fundraising event

Welcome

Check-in/New and good

Each member describes the best written or verbal invitation to a meeting or event that she or he ever received. Keep descriptions brief. Then each member should take a minute to talk about something new and good that has happened in his or her life since the last meeting.

Review the agenda

Group leader introduces the goal for the meeting: to plan a new fundraising event.

Review minutes from last meeting

Fundraising committee report

The committee tells the group how much money they will need to raise at the event

Budget pairing

The event budget for the year is presented, and the group breaks into pairs to discuss how much money should be spent on the new fundraising event. Comments and questions should then be discussed by the entire group.

Event planning training

A volunteer from a local public relations office conducts a 10-minute training on all of the elements to consider when planning an event (where to have it, whom to invite, program details, etc.).

Brief Q & A with the trainer

Brainstorm

Group leader passes out the "Tips for Brainstorming" handout, located at the end of this chapter, then briefly goes over its contents.

Small groups

Group leader initiates a group brainstorming session about what needs to be done: what the theme of the event should be and its name, where it should be held, whom should be invited, etc. Then the entire group splits into smaller groups to brainstorm each specific topic (entertainment, outreach, logistics, etc.).

Report back

Each small group presents its ideas.

Discussion

The entire group reconvenes to make comments and discuss questions.

Closing

Include time for highlights and appreciations.

Every meeting can have its boring or repetitive moments. Why not shake up your group with some completely new rules or strategies? Try these, taken from the April 1998 issue of *Inc.* magazine, and City Year, an innovative youth organization. Even if they are not appropriate for your group, they'll get you thinking about the type of innovations you may bring to your meetings:

Minutes

The Phelps Group, a Santa Monica-based marketing agency, conducts a section in their meetings called "minutes," a clarion call for brevity. Each of the teams in the company delivers a one-minute mini-lesson, teaching the group about some key piece of expertise, or perhaps handing out and summarizing a helpful article. There's also a "technology minute," a "grammar minute," (on the use of quotation marks, for instance) and an "office machine minute" (how to fix a photocopier jam).

The index card strategic plan

Can you imagine developing an entire strategic plan in silence? Well, it's been done. Key questions—What are the components of our mission? Who are our biggest competitors? In the next five years, what should be our priority goals?—are written on a flip chart and meeting participants are handed a stack of index cards. A facilitator points to the first question, and board members are off and writing. When they are done they move to the board and begin arranging their cards and others until they are satisfied with groupings, repeats, etc. Then it's on to the next question and the process is repeated. By the end of the meeting they've got a strategic plan in front of them. Of course, lots of refinement will follow, but they've gotten a good sense of the ideas and priorities of people in the room.

Ripples

City Year[1], a prominent national service program, is known for its "ripples." In meetings, individuals are regularly asked to share ways in which the organization has had some impact on the world around them. For example, one person's team member was accepted to the University of Rhode Island, while someone else overheard a person in the grocery store talking about how wonderful his recent Serve-a-thon experience was. Ripples are a great way for a meeting to start or end, and a great tool for keeping the group focused on the good work that is being accomplished.

[1] City Year, 285 Columbus Avenue, Boston, MA 02116. Phone: 617/927-2500.

11

Creating an Interactive Meeting

Answer the questions and use the suggestions in this section to help guide you as you work toward making your meetings more interactive.

• What are our goals for this meeting?

• What issues require member feedback?

• How can we strategically use the resources of this group?

• How can we let members know that their contributions count?

• How can we set up meetings so everyone is involved?

• Where in the agenda should we incorporate interactive activities?

• What is the goal of the interactive activities: team building, problem solving, or both?

• **Possible interactive strategies to use:**

    ☐ Check-ins   ☐ Brainstorming

    ☐ Talking in pairs   ☐ Appreciations

    ☐ Small groups   ☐ Go around at closing

    ☐ Games   ☐ Others:

- **Time:**

  When will the meeting be held?

  Is that a good time for most people? Keep school and work schedules in mind.

- **Place and space:**

  Plan for the following: access to the space, size of the space, kinds of movable furniture available, acoustics, cost, availability of parking, equipment, lighting, temperature control, and restroom facilities.

- **Resources available/needed:**

  ☐ Flip chart   ☐ Audio/visuals

  ☐ Art supplies   ☐ Game materials

  ☐ Room rental   ☐ Equipment rental

  ☐ Refreshments   ☐ Others: _____

- **Who will facilitate the process?**

- **Potential leadership roles for young people within the meeting:**

  ☐ Have young person present information

  ☐ Choose a young person to lead a committee

  ☐ Have young person direct a portion of the meeting

  ☐ Others:_____

- **Potential adult roles for the meeting:**

  ☐ Sitting next to young people so they are not isolated

  ☐ Making sure young people understand terminology used during the meeting

  ☐ Asking young people what they think/encouraging them to speak up

  ☐ Others:_____

Tips for Giving Appreciations

How often does it happen that you are plugging away at work, not getting enough done, and maybe even feeling a little hopeless about how much more you have to do? Then, someone walks by and says, "Hey! You're doing a really good job. Keep it up. It's making my job that much easier!" You return to your work, but the load feels a little lighter, things seem a bit more hopeful. That is the power of appreciation. Use it for yourself and for others.

Youth on Board suggests that you create a regular structured time for appreciations, because many work settings are just not in the habit of doing this kind of thing. If you plan to do this exercise with staff, board or council members, young people, or others, here are a few tips, adapted from publications of the Resource Center for Youth and Their Allies:

1. Don't put yourself down. For example, try not to say things like, "You're such a great runner. I couldn't run a block, but you're great."

2. When someone appreciates you, don't disagree with them. Just accept it.

3. Say your appreciation directly to the person who is being appreciated. "Jane, I want to appreciate you for..." It may be embarrassing, but it is more effective.

4. Laugh as much as you want! It helps with the awkwardness that most of us feel about giving and receiving appreciations.

5. Be as specific as possible. Use examples instead of just saying, "You're nice."

6. Stay away from compliments about a person's appearance, because those appreciations aren't as meaningful as others.

You don't have to know someone really well in order to appreciate them. Just tell them something you've noticed about them in the time that you've known them.

Tips for Brainstorming

How to brainstorm

• **Let the answers flow:** Once the brainstorm question is posed, allow yourself to say any answers that come to mind. Brainstorming is all about unclogging our thought processes and not censoring our ideas because we think they might be wrong.

• **Respect everyone's ideas:** No one in the group will make fun of or dismiss your ideas during a brainstorm. This is meant to be a process full of answers that you don't actually use, but saying these answers out loud allows you to play off of them and come up with whole new ideas.

• **Repeating is okay:** Even if you think your idea has already been said, don't be afraid to reiterate it or say it a little differently.

• **Answer now, evaluate later:** Wait until the entire group is done with the brainstorm before you start to evaluate it. While the brainstorm is going on, just focus on saying your answers.

Why brainstorm?

• **Free thinking:** Brainstorming allows you to run with your ideas, to free associate, and let new thoughts flow.

• **Group building:** Brainstorming gets a group thinking together. People play off of one another's ideas.

• **Everyone contributes:** Brainstorming gives everyone a chance to speak. People who are shy or more inhibited can speak out in the group without fear of judgment.

• **Cooperative product:** Brainstorming produces a list of ideas that don't belong to any one person. They belong to the entire group.

Develop a Mentoring Plan

This chapter reviews the need to develop a mentoring plan and offers ways to get things going. It also includes sample responsibilities and tips for mentors.

"My experience on the boards of progressive foundations has brought me into the same spaces with elders who are not only activists of the past, but are very much activists of the present and future. It is their longevity in the struggle, willingness to learn from young people, and humility about their contributions that have touched my life and have intensified my commitment to progressive movements for change."

— **Tram Nguyen**
honoree at Youth on Board's
Annual Strength in Numbers Event

Ms. Nguyen is one of many young people who have learned much from consistent contact and ongoing relationships with adults. Mentoring relationships on boards have an extra significance because young people and adults are working in the same arena. Young people can gain tremendous experience from having someone help them learn the ropes, navigate a system, and increase their effectiveness.

Modern-Day Mentoring

Traditionally, we think of mentoring relationships as working in one direction—a more experienced person giving knowledge to a novice in the field. That's fine if you're a 19th-century clockmaker, but in this day and age, both people need to be involved. Today's mentor doesn't dominate—he or she supports. The best mentors have two goals: to foster the development of new member's expertise through meaningful personal experiences, and to learn about themselves and develop their own skills by serving as mentors. That's right, mentors learn too!

Mentoring: A necessity for new members

When joining a group, new members of all ages can use the advice of a buddy who already knows the ropes. Young people are unique, however, because they seldom have prior professional experience. Mentors provide critical support to young people by helping them learn new terms, understand organizational culture, and build confidence to act as full partners in the group. These mentors only need be experienced, not *older*—young people can certainly mentor their peers.

Whether members of your group are under the age of 18, or their ages range from 13 to 60, mentoring is a great tool for inducting new members. It's important to note, however, that the wider the age range, the more important mentoring becomes. When joining mostly adult groups, young people face a unique and daunting challenge—entering an adult-dominated environment. Even though they may have the best of intentions, adults can seem intimidating to young people. Whether at home, at school, and/or at work, young people are accustomed to having adults govern their lives. It's a major shift for both young people and adults to think of one another as peers and partners, and establishing a mentoring program can help ease the transition.

Steps for Establishing a Mentoring Program

The following steps represent an ideal mentoring program. We acknowledge that all these steps need not be followed to establish a mentoring program that can work for your task force, council, board, or church vestry.

1) Designate a staff person who will match new members with mentors, coordinate meeting times, troubleshoot, and facilitate the overall process.

2) Be strategic as you match young people and mentors. Develop a list of criteria for mentors, based on their ability to relate to young people, their enthusiasm and patience, their knowledge base, and their overall personality. Remember, not everybody is suited to be a mentor.

3) Identify potential mentors and provide a brief training. Share the information listed in this chapter with your mentors.

4) Match mentors with new members and **plan a first meeting**. Make sure people exchange phone numbers at the end of the meeting so future meetings don't have to be coordinated through the central office. The designated staff person should simply supervise the relationships.

5) After a few mentor meetings, **do an informal evaluation** of the partnerships and hold a larger group meeting with all partners to discuss progress. If it is difficult to get the whole group together, conduct the evaluations in a small group format. This is a great chance to share insights from the individual relationships.

6) Mentors should **schedule regular check-ins** with new members to see how things are going. They can use the worksheet at the end of this chapter to structure these meetings. One of the primary functions of regular check-ins is to allow time for young people to tell their mentors what they need.

7) Stay flexible and patient. Mentoring programs require ongoing attention and adjustments. They are generally works in progress. If

> **Mentors provide critical support to young people by helping them learn new terms, understand organizational culture, and build confidence.**

12

new members are resistant to having a mentor, it might not be worth a push. Be sure you're clearly communicating the intent and function of the relationship, and then let the new members decide if it will work for them. Also, if one partnership doesn't seem to be working, try arranging another one. Don't become discouraged. Much of the success of mentor relationships depends on the chemistry between two individuals.

8) Don't forget parents and their critical role in young people's lives. **Encourage mentors to get to know parents** and build a strong relationship with them at the same time they are getting to know their child.

9) Mentors and new members, especially if the new members are young people, should **spend time together outside of meetings**. Spending informal time together gives mentors and new members time to get to know each other, laugh together, and feel comfortable with each other.

10) **Be a good sounding board**, but also encourage mentors and their advisees to work on problems together, rather than looking to you to "fix it."

Mentor Responsibilities

What follows is a list of suggested responsibilities for mentors. Consider those that make sense, given your schedule and your group's structure. However, points 2, 3, and 4 (regarding attendance, support, and orientation, respectively) should always be adhered to as closely as possible.

1. Build a relationship with the new member you are mentoring, especially if he or she is a young person. Spending informal time together, such as over lunch or at social events, gives mentors and new members time to get to know each other, laugh together, and feel comfortable with each other. Mentoring works best when it's not just about work.

2. Make sure young people know about and attend every meeting. This may mean making a reminder phone call. Many young people are not in the habit of carrying calendars. A special call from a mentor can be the deciding factor as to whether or not a young person attends a meeting, especially if you remind your advisee that *you* personally feel that having him or her there will make a big difference.

3. Support and encourage young people to participate during meetings. This can be done by simply asking them what they think about a particular issue or by sitting next to them during the meeting and quietly suggesting that they bring up helpful ideas or observations that they may have mentioned to you before. The more specific your questions, the more likely your advisee will feel comfortable answering them. For example, asking "What do you think we should do with our membership program" might not get much of a reply. Instead, ask "Do you think our membership program should include only young people, or both young people and young adults?"

4. Make sure that young people have been given a thorough orientation. They need to understand both the organization and their personal obligation. Once they are part of the group, arrange for ongoing trainings that might build their skills or help them further understand the function of your group.

5. Set aside some time before the young person's first board meeting to get to know one another. It also helps to initiate a relationship with your advisee's parents/guardians at this point.

6. If possible, meet with the youth before each meeting to prepare. This can be done a few days prior to the meeting or immediately before. It's also fine to prepare over the phone.

7. Debrief with your advisee after meetings whenever possible. Discuss highlights, ideas, and any concerns.

8. Communicate with the staff coordinator on a regular basis about how your mentor relationship is going.

9. Help young people get onto committees. Once they are on committees, help involve them in the work of that group.

10. Help young people follow-up on the commitments they make during meetings. You may want to help them locate information they need, or help them organize materials and thoughts.

11. Get into it! Mentoring is more than fulfilling a list of responsibilities. Even if it gets tough, stick with it. When you are facing challenges, remember the reason you are doing it—you really care about the success of young people in your group.

Some advice for mentors

Your role is both fun and challenging. You want to convey your knowledge and expertise, yet do so in a way that will encourage young people to build on their own experiences. Perhaps it is best to think of yourself as a guide instead of a teacher— helping young people as they gain their own knowledge about decision making. You can foster this unique relationship in several ways:

• Convey your respect to the young people with whom you work.

• Listen as much as you speak.

• Know that you have as much to learn from young people as they do from you.

• Ask for young people's opinions.

• Ask for feedback and offer feedback on your mentoring relationship.

• Understand that most young people find *all* adults intimidating. Try to stay approachable and treat them as peers.

So You've Got Yourself a Mentor

Unlike most other youth/adult relationships, your mentor's job is to serve you! However, remember that the person you've been paired with is working to help you figure things out for yourself, not just give you easy answers. You can make this partnership work by doing several things:

- **Trust your adult mentor.**

  She or he definitely knows things that will be helpful to you as a member of this group.

- **Ask lots of questions when you're confused.**

  There is a lot of new information for you to pick up. It will take active participation from you to learn it.

- **Speak up when you have an opinion.**

  You know things that no one else in your group knows. Your insights are unique. Share them with everybody.

- **Remember** that by taking on this decision-making position, you are part of a larger movement—one that is working to gain respect for young people and to make their voices heard in communities and organizations of all kinds. You are a powerful leader!

Mentoring for Meetings

Consider this list of suggestions for mentors in governing-structure settings, developed in collaboration with Community Partnerships with Youth, Fort Wayne, IN.

Preparing for the meeting

The mentor and youth should meet before each meeting and:

- Each share a "new and good" to start. A new and good is something good that has happened in your life recently, and it helps us remember things that *are* going well and provides an opportunity to get to know each other better.

- Review the agenda for the meeting, discussing any questions.

- Discuss possible contributions and views on agenda items.

- Plan for the young person's participation, remembering that his/her input is essential.

- Set goals for the meeting, such as having the young person speak up about **at least three** agenda items.

At the first meeting

- The mentor introduces the young person to as many members as possible before the meeting, and introduces her or him to the group at the outset of the meeting.

- The young person talks about his or herself during the introduction. Make sure there is plenty of preparation time, so he or she isn't put on the spot.

- All members should give quick introductions of themselves.

- Members should wear nametags.

After all meetings

The mentor and young person should meet after each meeting to debrief. Possible questions for the mentor to ask follow below. You may want to consider having the new member actually write down her or his answers:

- What were some of the highlights of the meeting? What did you learn?

- Did you find the meeting interesting?

- What questions do you have about the discussion?

- How would you rate group interaction during the meeting?

- What questions or observations do you have about the way the meeting was run?

- What could have been done to help the meeting to run better?

- Did you feel comfortable participating in the meeting?

- What did you like about your participation in the meeting?

- Did you feel like people were paying attention to what you had to say?

- Did you feel as if you were being treated differently than anyone else?

- What would you like to do differently in future meetings?

- What information do you need to help you participate more fully?

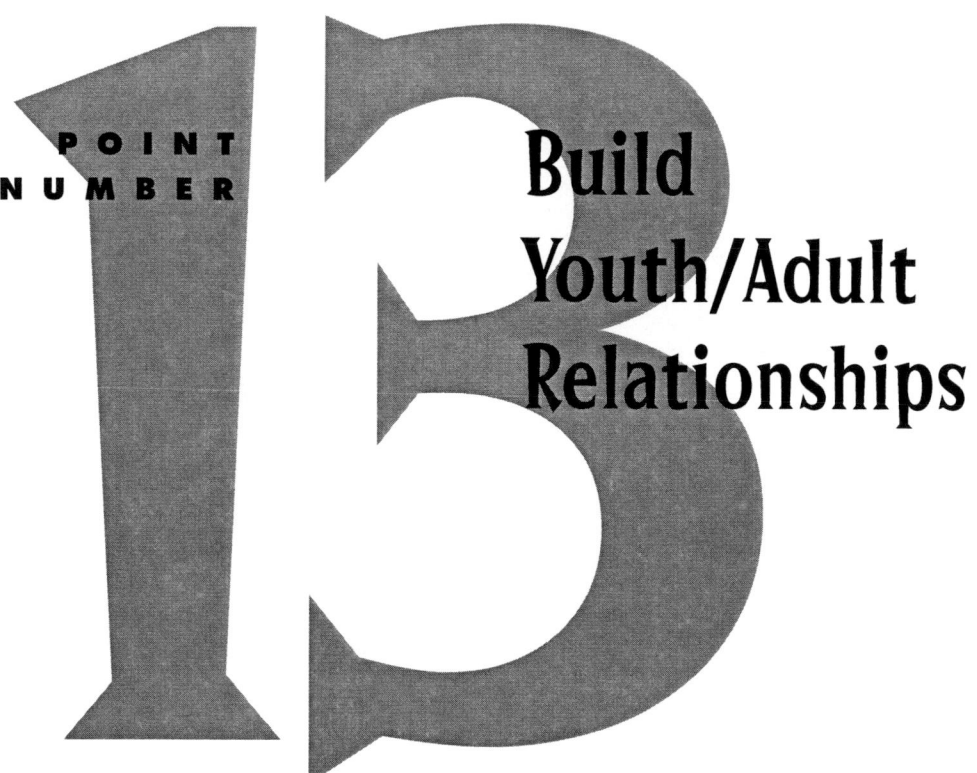

Build Youth/Adult Relationships

This chapter outlines strategies for developing strong youth/adult relationships, which are key to successfully involving youth in decision making. It also provides information on how to support young people in all aspects of their lives.

Why the emphasis on relationships? Because working with youth in governance and the lives of these youth in general are connected.[1] Young people are learning about life in everything that they do, including the work they do with you. Your work together will go better if you get to know the *whole* young person— the one he or she is beyond your organization's projects. During their formative years, youth need guidance and assistance. People in general will make big changes in their lives when they can tell that someone cares about them. Strong, respectful relationships with adults and with each other give young people the safety and confidence to lead in their communities and transform their own lives.

All successful community-change programs work because of peoples' relationships with each other. From a local community effort to build a youth center to the international movement to end apartheid, it is the relationships that create social change. This human caring is where deep, permanent transformation comes from. The same is true for working with young people and involving them in the decision-making processes of your organization. Programs in any setting will usually function better and lead to life-changing experiences when they are based on caring, committed relationships.

For some adults, the idea of befriending young people sounds unprofessional—they think working and being involved in young

> **All successful community-change programs work because of peoples' relationships with each other.**

---

[1] The majority of the text in this chapter was taken from the Resource Center for Youth and their Allies pamphlet *Building Relationships* and from the pamphlet *Understanding and Supporting Young People* by Jenny Sazama.

13

people's lives outside of work should be two separate things. This division is counterproductive. "Professional distance" keeps us separate from young people. You can't just expect a young person to work hard without getting to know them . From helping them fill out college applications to offering tips for a driving test, youth need adults to be supportive in all aspects of their lives. It's not wrong to want to help them.

And remember that building relationships with young people is not a one-way street—it benefits both young people *and* adults. It's easy to fall into the trap of thinking that assisting young people is a "sacrifice" that you are making for their benefit. But like white people reaching out to people of color in order to lend them a "helping hand," this reasoning is flawed. Adults are not "better than" young people. The truth is, building relationships with youth will give adults people skills that can transfer to almost anything they do. Adults gain part of their ability to function in this increasingly diverse world by learning to relate to a large and important segment of our population.

Tips for Cultivating Leadership

There are a host of ways you can cultivate youth leadership by developing strong relationships with the youth in your organization or community. Here are a few tips and suggestions that were developed by the Resource Center for Youth and Their Allies after interviewing more than 500 young people worldwide.

Let young people be in charge.

The best way for young people to learn is by doing. Allow them to make important telephone calls, to take charge of planning events, to facilitate meetings, etc. Your role is to supply encouragement and have confidence in them so they believe they are fully capable of handling any task. Additionally, you should be ready to assist young people when and where they are in need. While it is a good idea to try to match young people's strengths with the tasks you ask them to perform, recognize that some may need a push in the right direction while others will not recognize that they need help.

Remember that you do not always know better.

Lack of experience is often an excuse for trivializing the input of young people. While you may have more information about some issues, remember that, in many situations, young people truly know what's best for young people. Lack of experience does not indicate a lack of intelligence. In that same vein, remember not to force your opinions on young people or dominate conversations. The more you can sit back and listen and let young people test their ideas and thinking, the faster they will feel confident about their own thinking.

The best way for young people to learn is by doing.

Remember the importance of involving parents.

Parents will seldom let their sons and daughters participate in activities that they do not understand. It is extremely important to include parents right from the start. Get to know them. Share information with them. Answer their questions. Invite them to events. Appreciate them and the work that their child is doing for your group. Convey to them your enthusiasm for the work you're doing. In addition, let young people know that you are going to be talking to their parents. Let them know that you are not checking up on them or breaking any confidentiality, but that talking with their parents will insure that they know how important young people are to your organization.

Consistency and commitment are key.

When you make a commitment to a young person or a group of young people, it is important to be clear about what that

13

commitment will involve and then stick to it. Even if all young people don't attend meetings or events, be sure that you are there. Young people have a lot of inconsistency in their lives. It means a lot to them if you demonstrate that you will always follow through with what you say.

Never believe that young people don't have an opinion.

You might have to ask young people to express their ideas many different ways before what they really want to say comes out, but don't dismiss a young person's opinion. Young people's opinions are disregarded so often that they may not believe that you really want to take them seriously. When given information and time to consider the issues, along with the expectation that they have something valuable to contribute, young people will come up with good ideas for almost any situation.

Speak to young people with respect.

Always speak to young people with the utmost respect. If you can show them that you value their opinions, they will listen carefully to you and take seriously what you have to say. Be aware of the tendency of adults to speak to young people in a different tone of voice. If you've spoken to a young person in a way that may have been construed as condescending, don't pretend that it didn't happen. Simply apologize. It will be much appreciated.

Meet young people on their turf.

Young people are often asked to be part of the adult world. Most of their time—in school, in youth programs, at home—is controlled by our standards. When we want to know how their day was, we expect them to come sit at the dinner table and tell us in ways that make us feel comfortable. Instead, why not try to talk to them where they hang out? Try talking in the food court at the mall, between video games at the arcade, or in the crowd at a sporting

If you can show young people that you value their opinions, they will listen carefully to you and take seriously what you have to say.

event. If we can reverse the power dynamic so that we show respect for and value their world, trust will come more easily.

Don't forget to have some fun.

Young people are full of life. They love to have fun. As adults, we often feel that we have to be serious in order to accomplish anything educational. With young people, it's often more effective to make all activities fun. As young people have put it, "Learn to relax around us; we don't bite."

Intervene when necessary.

If a young person is having a personal crisis, such as a breakup with a significant other, a problem with alcohol or drugs, etc., you have an opportunity to let that young person know that you care. Any boundaries that might have separated you before are now weakened—she or he needs you. Consider ways you can offer support without being invasive; commitment and trust will usually follow.

Give young people space to grow.

The young people in your group may not be at the point where they can take on total leadership. Be sure not to underestimate what they can do, but also don't push a young person who isn't ready into a leadership role. Talk with them about what is important to them, and what skills they want to develop. Have patience, too. Sometimes it takes a young person several months in a new environment before they really act like themselves. Only ask a young person to lead if you have confidence that she or he can succeed, with your support.

Help young people to rely on each other.

Adults cannot empower young people on their own. Young people will never truly be powerful until they can rely on each other, value each other's opinions, and help each other. To that end, it's important for adults to help young people in their relationships with each other. When you observe unhealthy competition and insulting language or behavior, thoughtfully but firmly interrupt. Encourage young people to give specific positive feedback to each other, as well as offer growth and improvement suggestions to each other and to you. Young people can learn much from one another.

Allow young people to be discouraged.

While it would be wonderful if we could fix everything for young people, we can't. They must figure out things for themselves. If we can listen to their frustrations without judgment, they will be able to come to the solutions that make the most sense for them. Be confident that they will find solutions, but at the same time, show that you are concerned and leave them room to express their feelings.

Form an informal young people's "advisory board" for yourself.

If you have an opportunity to develop relationships with young people outside your group, do so. Getting to know young people informally will help in your more formal relations with the youth in your group. However, don't discount having both formal and informal relationships with the youth on your board.

Don't be afraid to make mistakes.

You will make mistakes; it's inevitable. Given this, why not try to delight in your mistakes? Make fun of them. Don't try to cover them up, apologize for them, or explain them away. The less defensive you can be, the more quickly mistakes diffuse. It's important to show young people that you are willing to take risks, and that you can handle mistakes with humor and honesty.

Be open about you.

Share your experiences with young people, including the current struggles and successes in your life. Adults often feel that relationships with young people need to be only one way. It helps build trust and commitment to the group if young people feel that they matter in your life.

Listening to Young People

Adults can begin to break down barriers by learning to listen well to young people. Listening can also be used to help young people build relationships with each other. There are many ways to use listening in your work with young people, only two of which are explained in detail below. One way is to listen to the young people around you in your everyday interactions. A second way, which we call *listening appointments*, is to establish specific times where listening is the only activity. *Special time* combines individual listening with a fun activity.

Listening appointments

These are specific times that you set aside to get together with a young person and listen to her or him on a more in-depth level. It can be anywhere from a half-hour to two hours. It helps to decide together on a specific amount of time at the beginning. Carefully listen to the young person talk about whatever he or she chooses. If you have specific issues that you know the youth has been dealing with, it's alright to bring those up, but from there on let the young person speak. In normal conversations or in meetings, we usually listen casually, jumping in to offer our comments whenever we think of something to say. The listening referred to here is different. Listen as the young person unfolds her or his thoughts, without interruption, interpretation, or judgment. If you can listen

13

to a young person and help her or him think without directing the conversation or giving advice, he or she will arrive at possible solutions. As always, keep the situations and feelings discussed strictly confidential.

Special time

Combining listening with social time works well. Let the young person be in charge of where you go or what you do. This is one time where the young person gets to reverse the power dynamic. By doing this, you are giving a young person a unique experience that will change their perspective. Take an interest in what young people like to do with their free time. You can also offer to help with homework, or even offer to get them home safely after meetings. Any way that you can show you care what happens to young people outside of meeting settings will make a difference.

We're All Individuals

Just as with anyone else, when forging relationships with young people, it is important to keep in mind that each one is a unique individual. They may have age in common, and dress and talk alike, but the similarities might end there. Be that as it may, there are a few things that adults should keep in mind about specific groups of young people.

Class background

One of the ways that class background becomes an issue is through the fact that people in general are trained to think that accent and grammar reflect intelligence. This stereotype confuses all of us, regardless of our class background. Keep in mind that one idiom is no better than another. We should delight in all the different ways people speak. If a young person's vernacular is different than yours, try learning it, with humor and respect, as doing so may put young people at ease.

Young men

Boys lose human contact and closeness very early. They are expected to be strong enough to figure things out for themselves. Young men then begin to believe this and act like they don't want or need anything from anyone. People are often scared of them and believe the rough facade young men are taught to show to the world. It's important to relate to what young men are going through, and support them though they may have a hard time talking about their lives.

Young women

Young women are often expected to need help. People often worry about them and think that they can't take care of themselves. Even the strongest young women believe on some level that their success is dependent on what other people think about them. Notice when young women are quiet, and encourage them to speak their minds about everything. In group settings, encourage everyone to say something, even if it's just a few words about their day. Remember that young women have a lot to say.

Other groups

It also helps to be sensitive to issues other than those outlined above, including gay/lesbian/bisexual/transgender young people and disabled young people, as you work toward befriending young people.

> **In group settings, encourage everyone to say something, even if it's just a few words about their day.**

Wendy Schaetzel Lesko says working with young people is as satisfying as "having a delicious meal every day." Wendy is the founder and executive director of the Activism 2000 Project[2], and has been a youth advocate since the 10th grade. Now, as an adult of 49 years, she says the trick to working with young people is not to approach the work from the perspective of being an older person trying to immerse yourself in youth culture, or trying to take a psychological approach to understanding how young people think. "What I can do is be completely myself, be honest, and have good ears," Wendy says. Successful adult/youth partnerships are really about adults respecting and enjoying young people, Wendy says, because, after all, young people are people, just like anyone else.

In addition to the respect factor, adults need to realize that working with youth involves a difference in adult behavior. "It means not having meetings at 10 a.m.," Wendy says. "It means not having boring meetings. It means being up-front and not having hidden agendas." Adults must also be mindful that they can open doors for young news- and decision-makers by identifying timely opportunities, introducing them to key policy makers and media representatives, and networking them with other decision makers.

As for the most challenging part of her job, Wendy says it's convincing young people that fighting with those in power for what youth believe in is worth their time. "Young people bring so many issues to life," she says, and they have "real power to motivate or shame." As young people tell her, they need adults to help build on their ideas, not to patronize them.

[2] See the *Resource Directory*, located at the end of this book, for Activism 2000 Project contact information.

Create
Support
Networks

This chapter guides adults through the process of creating a support network with young people, and doing the same for themselves.

With all you've been given to think about and do through the first 13 points of this book, the information in this final point is the key to holding everything together. We at Youth on Board find that, for the young leaders and adult allies doing this work, it is crucial to get together and talk about their lives. When individuals gather in a structured setting to discuss their experiences, the actual work that they do together, whether they be young people or adults, progresses more smoothly. We believe that support networks should not be treated as an optional idea. Remember that this work requires us to strike a healthy balance between assisting young people and taking care of ourselves and each other.

Creating a Resource Group to Network Young Leaders

Young people are inherently intelligent, cooperative, and caring. When given the proper encouragement, they will flourish. What follows are some guidelines that have been used by adults to help them effectively assist young people. As you work to have strong relationships with young people, be mindful of the relationships that they build with other youth. Young people who are on boards of directors, advisory boards, or in other leadership positions can provide excellent support for one another. By being networked with other youth leaders, young people see that they are not alone in their work and that other youth care about the same issues. They also discover that their peers are facing similar issues—not being taken seriously by adults, getting bored during meetings, or feeling left out of pre-meeting conversations. This support is the type that only young people can provide to one another.

Finding ways to bring young leaders together is extremely important. You can have meetings with the youth serving in governance positions within your organization or group, even if it's only two young people. They can provide invaluable support to each other. Or, you can create a group consisting of youth outside of your organization—there are many young people out there in leadership positions.

At Youth on Board, we have organized monthly youth resource group meetings for young leaders. A resource group is a structured meeting of people who listen and talk about the things that matter to them. We don't use group time to do much skills-based work; we use it instead to listen to each other and offer support. As they get to know each other, group members can develop an understanding and appreciation for the great work that each person does, and discover ways of learning from each other's struggles and successes. In addition, resource group work can teach participants skills that help them offer effective support for other group members and for the people with whom they work.

If you would like to build a youth resource group, the following steps will help you do so (these same steps can also be used to form an adult resource group). There is no magic in the structure we propose, although many years of experimentation are behind these recommendations. The real key to an effective resource group is the quality of listening that you, as the initial facilitator of the group, are able to foster. Certain habits, such as interrupting a speaker and offering advice or analysis, will creep into people's interaction in the group. It will be your job to steer people back to focused listening, so that a real sense of safety and respect have a chance to

Resource group work can teach participants skills that help them offer effective support for other group members and for the people with whom they work.

develop. Once the group is well established, a young person should take over the role of facilitator.

Here's how to set up a youth resource group:

Gather interested people. To begin, think about whom you want to bring together. Questions such as "Which people would enjoy each other's company?" "Who could learn from each other?" and "What size group is manageable?" must be considered.

Select a volunteer co-facilitator. Ask a young person or two to assist you for the first few meetings. Eventually, the resource group should be run by a young person. A youth resource group should be a place where young people can lead *and* learn.

Choose people who can listen to others. Since the group will have listening skills at its center, every member should be able to offer respect and attention to others.

Start with a small group if necessary. The quality of interaction is far more important to the success of the group than its size. Three or four people getting together regularly can become a very effective resource group. As the people in a small group strengthen their relationships, they will attract others, and your group will grow.

Be creative about meeting times and places. Do weeknights work for everyone, or would weekend afternoons work better? Meetings can take place over meals and in public places with private spaces, such as restaurants and some libraries.

Decide how often you will meet. This decision is an important one. Here is a brief summary of Youth on Board's experience with various meeting frequencies:

• Once-a-week meetings have many advantages. People get to know each other quickly, and their sense of camaraderie isn't lost between meetings. And group members begin to get a sense of the ongoing sagas in each other's leadership experiences.

- Every-other-week meetings can also allow people to develop familiarity with each other's issues. However, the sense of continuity is harder to capture. We recommend that an every-other-week group begin by meeting four to six weeks in a row to jumpstart the process.

- Monthly meetings can work, but we have found that relationships take much longer to build, especially if your group is composed of young leaders who are new to each other. Again, if you can only meet monthly, begin by holding weekly meetings for the first four to six weeks.

Remind each member of the meeting by telephone a day ahead of time. Your call will help group members prioritize activities around your group meeting. A phone call is also an opportunity to remind people that you think their contributions are valuable.

Format for resource group meetings

Now that you've gathered your resource group, it's time to think about a format for your meetings. At the first meeting, we suggest that you clarify for everyone the goals of the group. You might quickly verbalize introductory information, or sum things up on a flyer you hand out. Even if you use written information, people will appreciate hearing *your* reasons for starting the group. Also during your first meeting, establish the guidelines for the group. It's important that everyone understand that they will be learning how to form listening relationships within the group, which are different from their casual friendships. Have participants practice their first listening partnership—groups of no more than three people where each person is listened to for five minutes, uninterrupted. In order to develop the kind of focused attention the resource group is striving to achieve, there are a few general guidelines for the group to remember:

- Give your full attention to the person who is speaking—do not interrupt.

- Do not offer advice. Instead, offer an attitude of trust in each person's ability to think, experiment, and problem-solve.

- Openly praise the good you see in yourself, and in others.

- Keep the situations discussed in the group strictly confidential. Don't refer to what someone has said in the group when it's your turn to talk at the end of the meeting, or when you meet on other occasions.

Lastly, have the group brainstorm specific topics for discussion during this and the next few meetings. You can suggest topics, such as opinions on high school shootings or life-changing experiences, or gather ideas from the "Principles for Young People" worksheet, located in *Point 10: Conduct Intergenerational Training*, but it's best to let the group decide on what they want to discuss. Once topics have been selected, divide them among members who agree to give brief general presentations on each topic. The presentation should include a list of discussion questions. One topic will be presented at each meeting, or as needed, and brainstorming sessions should be held as often as needed.

After the first one, your meetings should take on a regular format. We recommend the following:

Greetings: Each person who comes deserves a personal welcome. At first, it takes the leader's initiative to set the tone. Participants' warmth toward each other will increase as they become more comfortable.

> **A phone call is also an opportunity to remind people that you think their contributions are valuable.**

What's going well? When all members have arrived, each person should give a brief account of what's going well in his or her leadership experience. This simple way of beginning a resource group meeting helps shift their focus from their unsolved problems to their victories, which are all too often ignored. Encourage members who can't think of anything good to keep reaching for the bright side of a bad situation.

Presentation: The designated young person gives her or his presentation on the topic predetermined at the first meeting. Encourage group members to jot down any questions that may arise for them during the presentation.

Small group discussion: Members divide into groups of no more than three to exchange listening time of at least five minutes on the topic of the meeting. This listening time helps each person sort through a few of the many issues and events he or she has yet to talk enough about.

Group attention for each person: This time is the core of any resource group. Young people can share personal stories pertaining to the topic of the meeting, or talk about issues that may have come up during the small group discussions. It is important that each person be given the opportunity to use the attention of the entire group, and that the time allotted to each person be approximately equal. This equal time principle keeps a group from falling into patterns already established in our society, which grant people who talk a lot more attention than those who hesitate to speak or who think before they speak.

Appreciations: At the close of the meeting, ask each person to offer specific appreciations of someone in the group. It's important that nobody go home having been left out at appreciations time, so you might ask that people appreciate their small group partner(s), or appreciate someone who hasn't yet been appreciated. Help

It is important that each person be given the opportunity to use the attention of the entire group, and that the time allotted to each be approximately equal.

group members keep their appreciations "clean" by asking them not to mention what a person worked on during his or her turn. An example of a clean appreciation is, "Elena is such a brave young woman. I love how she takes on challenges." Conversely, an inappropriate appreciation would be something like, "Joel is amazing. If I had to deal with all the stuff he has to deal with, I'd have gone bonkers by now. I wonder where he gets the courage that I don't seem to have." The difference between these two appreciations is important. Everyone will benefit from being required to appreciate each other without put-downs or comparisons that undermine their own self-respect. Remember, appreciations are done because people have gone out on a limb to talk about themselves. Appreciations are not some form of deciding who's "best." For more appreciation tips, see the handout at the end of *Point 11: Make Meetings Work*.

Adult-to-Adult Support

It is not easy to remember that you need support too. As adults working with youth, we tend to put ourselves and our own personal growth on the back burner. Just as youth need the support of other youth, executive directors, board chairs, and other adults managing intergenerational groups need opportunities to talk with one another about their experiences. They need a forum for comparing stories, discussing difficult issues that arise, talking about successes, and supporting one another. Adult-to-adult support is also important because it helps governing structures move past the points where they get stuck or feel burned out. It also helps us "walk the talk"— how can we ask youth to work together if we do not do so ourselves?

Designing adult allies meetings

The best way to develop an adult network is to host meetings among those people who are working to increase youth leadership and governance in their organizations and councils. You may want to consider a two-hour breakfast meeting (often mornings are the best times for people with busy schedules), or perhaps an after-work casual dinner where people can get to know each other informally and discuss issues that are emerging in their groups.

Whatever form your meeting takes, we recommend that you include a bit of formal programming. It helps to have a some concrete talking points. (The "Principles for Allies to Young People" worksheet at the end of this chapter can help you think of topics to discuss.) Open the meeting by going around the room and having each person say what's exciting about involving young people in governance. Use the following discussion points and the attached worksheet to develop material for the heart of the meeting. You may also want to review the organizational assessment checklist found in *Point 2: Conduct an Organizational Assessment,* and discuss ways of moving your organizations forward in any of the areas listed.

Discussion points for adult allies meetings:

- Why are youth members important to your organization? Why did you decide to include youth in the governance of your organization?

- What is working successfully for your organization? How do you see youth benefiting from the work you do?

- How have various organizations dealt with legal issues around youth governance?

- How do you keep meetings interactive?

- Does your organization have an orientation program in place for new members? If so, what form does it take?

- What are the pros and cons of establishing a mentor program? What other ways can we support young members?

- What have been the biggest obstacles to youth participation in your organization, and how have you overcome them?

- Burnout: how do you deal with it, and how can we avoid it?

- What was your life like when you were younger? How can our past experiences help us in our present work?

A thorough explanation of how to facilitate a resource group is given in the Resource Center for Youth and their Allies 20-page booklet, *Leading a Resource Group*, which is available through Youth on Board. The majority of text in this chapter came from this booklet.

Principles for Allies of Young People

Items on this list, compiled as part of Youth on Board's SureShot workshop, might remind you of <u>you</u> at your best. Briefly describe instances when you have followed several of the principles listed below.

Supporting Yourself and Other Adults

Take pride in being an adult. Enjoy the age you are. Consider the things you really like about adulthood. We have to enjoy our own lives before we can help others with theirs.

_____

_____

_____

Recognize that just being an adult can be intimidating. It's not your fault, but the simple fact that you are an adult can intimidate many young people. To be a good ally, you need to recognize the power difference between the generations. Since adults often have the upper hand, it is important to know when to listen and let young people have their say.

_____

_____

_____

Spread the word. You can talk about it. You can print it. You can yell from the rooftops! Just let people know that youth have great insights and that they should be at the center of our communities and our lives.

_____

_____

_____

Organize other adults. Arrange workshops, retreats, and other gatherings for adults to learn about youth as decision makers. Be sure to consult with young people for guidance in the process.

_____

_____

_____

Collaborate with other adults. Work together on behalf of young people. Move past the drive to compete. Allies can be much more effective if they collaborate and build on one another's strengths.

_____

_____

_____

_____

Stop adultism. Adultism is the negative stereotyping of young people. When you see it in action, take a stand against it. This means both within institutions and among individuals. The idea of speaking up can be frightening, but if you do it with concern and respect, people will generally be receptive.

_____

_____

_____

_____

Supporting Young People

Remember your younger years. Adults seldom take time to remember their teen years. However, when supporting young people, you should try to remember the challenges, joys, concerns, and interests you had at their age.

_____

_____

_____

Be a committed part of young people's lives. Earn the trust and friendship of young people by being a stable and constant part of their lives.

_____

_____

_____

Remind youth of their importance. Help young people remember that their involvement is both important and achievable. Because they are dismissed so frequently, they sometimes forget just how much they know. It helps to point out young people's successes.

_____

_____

_____

_____

Hold high expectations of young people. Expect the young people with whom you work to have respect for themselves and for one another. They should be proud and confident in their thinking.

_____

_____

_____

_____

Help youth support one another. Sometimes the best support a young person can have is from another young person, but they don't always know this. Because young people have learned to distrust themselves, they have also learned to distrust their peers.

_____

_____

_____

Be a guide, not a boss. When working with young people, adults tend to run to polar extremes. They either try to control everything, or they become too permissive, leaving every decision to young people. Working with youth is a balancing act. Be careful to guide young people without taking control.

_____

_____

_____

Resource Directory

Activism 2000 Project

Encourages young people to speak up about issues they care about. Offers books, videos, training, and consulting on youth participation in decision-making processes and free materials and technical assistance to young people on how to move their ideas into action.

> P.O. Box E
> Kensington, MD 20895
> 1-800-KID-POWER
> www.youthactivism.com

Center for Youth as Resources

Provides small grants to youth and supports them as they design and implement issue-related projects. Past organizational and youth participants help provide training and technical assistance.

> 1700 K Street, NW, Suite 801
> Washington, DC 20006
> 202/261-4185
> www.yar.org

Barry Checkoway

Has career commitment to creating community change through research, teaching and training, and consultation and technical assistance. His research includes studies of increasing involvement of traditionally under-served people worldwide through multicultural community organizations, social planning, and urban neighborhood work.

> 2846 School of Social Work Building
> 1080 South University Ave.
> Ann Arbor, MI 48109-1106
> 734/763-5960
> barrych@umich.edu

Coalition of Community Foundations for Youth

Strengthens the leadership capacity of community foundations to improve the lives of children, youth, and families.

> 1000 Broadway, Suite 302
> Kansas City, MO 64105-1540
> 816/842-4246

The Comfort Zone

Provides resources, publications, and networks to help young people make positive and creative choices about their lives and their money.

P.O. Box 336
North Cambridge, MA 02140
617/573-9731

Community Partnerships With Youth, Inc.

Has developed a training curriculum and provides training to young people about their role as trustee, or as partners in the governance process.

6319 Constitution Drive
Fort Wayne, IN 46804
219/436-4402
www.cpyinc.org

Constitutional Rights Foundation

The mission of CRF is to be activists for the rights of young people.

601 South Kingsley Drive
Los Angeles, CA 90005
213/487-5590
www.crf-usa.org

Council of Michigan Foundations

An association of more than 430 foundations and corporations that make grants for charitable purposes and whose mission it is to enhance, improve, and increase philanthropy in Michigan.

One S. Harbor Avenue, Suite 3
Grand Haven, MI 49417
616/842-7080
www.cmif.org

Do Something

Through its BRICK Awards program, funds innovative projects started by community activists under the age of 30.

423 West 55th Street
8th Floor
New York, NY 10019
212/523-1175
www.dosomething.org

Girls Incorporated

A national youth organization dedicated to helping every girl become strong, smart, and bold.

> Girls Incorporated
> 120 Wall Street
> New York, NY 10005-3902
> 800/221-2606
> www.girlsincofalbany.org

Midwest Academy

A training institute for progressive organizers and activists that conducts six to eight week-long training sessions yearly.

> 225 W. Ohio, Suite 250
> Chicago, IL 60610
> 312/645-6010

The National Assembly of Health and Human Service Organizations, Inc.

Advances the effectiveness of each member and provides collective leadership in the areas of health and human service.

> 1319 F Street, NW, Suite 601
> Washington, DC 20004
> 202/347-2080
> www.nassembly.org

National 4-H Council, At The Table

At The Table seeks to advance the youth in governance movement on a national level. They maintain a database of organizations with youth board members and resources related to youth in governance.

> 7100 Connecticut Avenue
> Chevy Chase, MD 20815
> 301/961-2972
> www.fourhcouncil.edu

National Center for Nonprofit Boards

Dedicated to increasing the effectiveness of nonprofit organizations by strengthening their boards of directors.

> 1828 L Street, NW, Suite 900
> Washington, DC 20036-5104
> 800/883-6262
> www.ncnb.org

National Youth Leadership Council, Strategic Youth Initiatives

Provides training and technical assistance related to youth leadership and service-learning. Each training is developed to meet the needs of the client and is lead by at least one adult in partnership with at least one young person.

> 1910 West Country Road B
> St. Paul, MN 55113
> 651/631-3672
> www.nylc.org

New York State Youth Council

Has resources on how to develop a youth council and create working relationships between youth and adults.

> 52 Washington Street
> Rensselaer, NY 12144

Office of the Superintendent of Public Instruction, Youth Leadership and Service Initiative

Encourages youth involvement in service-learning in schools and communities.

> PO Box 47200
> Olympia, WA 98501
> 360/753-2858

Points of Light Foundation

Works with leaders to maximize efforts in community volunteering. Its Youth Outreach area provides training and technical assistance to young people and organizations to develop programs that involve young people as leaders.

> 1400 I Street, NW, Suite 800
> Washington, DC 20005
> 202/729-8000
> www.pointsoflight.org

Promise Project

Offers publications, training, and consultation to help groups create successful youth/adult partnerships within the greater Kansas City area.

> YMCA of Greater Kansas City
> 3100 Broadway, #930
> Kansas City, MO 64111
> 861/561-9622
> www.ymca-kc.org

Re-evaluation Counseling

A process whereby people of all ages and of all backgrounds can learn how to exchange effective help with each other in order to free themselves from the effects of past distress experiences.

> 719 2nd Avenue
> Seattle, WA 98109
> 206/284-0311
> www.rc.org

Resource Center for Youth and their Allies (RCYA)

Provides information, training, and technical assistance to young people and their allies. RCYA is closely affiliated with Youth on Board.

> 25 Boylston Street
> Jamaica Plain, MA 02130
> 617/522-5560

Resource Development Institute

Provides evaluation consulting services, helping organizations to improve programs and build resources.

> 601 Walnut
> Kansas City, MO 64106
> 816/221-5000
> www.rdikc.org

S.C.A.L.E.

Student Coalition for Action in Literacy Education is a national network of college students, faculty, administrators, community leaders, and new readers working to help create and support campus-based literacy programs.

> CB#3505
>
> University of North Carolina at Chapel Hill
>
> 140 E. Franklin Street
>
> Chapel Hill, NC 27599
>
> 919/962-1542

Washington Youth Voice Project ESD 112

Works to strengthen youth involvement in schools and communities by helping students and adults gain the skills and resources needed to work together effectively and efficiently.

> 2500 NE 65th Avenue
>
> Vancouver, WA 98661-6812
>
> 360/750-7500 x362
>
> www.esd112.webnet.edu

YouthBuild USA

Encourages youth to take charge of their lives and gain skills that lead to economic independence, while helping rebuild their communities.

> 58 Day Street
>
> P.O. Box 440322
>
> Somerville, MA 02144
>
> 617/623-9900
>
> www.youthbuild.org

Youth as Resources

Connects youth to their communities to improve community life nationally and internationally through the spread of youth-led service initiatives.

> 1700 K Street, NW, 2nd Floor
>
> Washington, DC 20006-3817
>
> 202/261-4185
>
> www.ncpc.org

Youth Leadership Institute

A community-based institute that joins with young people to build communities that value, honor, and support youth. Offers a wide array of programs, all of which are grounded in a positive youth development philosophy.

> 870 Market Street, Suite 708
> San Francisco, CA 94102
> 415/397-2256

Youth on Board

Provides training, consultation, and publications on how to involve young people in decision making. Emphasizes building effective relationships between adults and young people. We have several training resources for individuals and groups, ranging from two-hour introductory sessions to week-long train-the-trainer courses. Our SureShot introductory workshop guides groups of adults and young people through key concepts of youth in decision making, including action plans for involving youth in governance. We also offer skills training for young people to prepare them for leadership positions through our SpringBoard workshop series. All of our seminars emphasize the importance of developing strong, supportive relationships between adults and young people as a key element in the success of youth-involvement programs. In addition to our workshops, we offer customized technical assistance for organizations and individuals.

> 58 Day Street
> P.O. Box 440322
> Somerville, MA 02144
> 617/623-9900 x1242
> www.youthonboard.org

14 Points: Successfully Involving Youth in Decision Making

Order Form

Please send me ____ copies of *14 Points: Successfully Involving Youth in Decision Making* for **$25** per copy plus a **$4.50** shipping and handling charge for the first book and **$1** for each additional book.

Please send me ____ copies of the video *At The Table: Youth Voices in Decision Making Part 1 & Part* for **$19.95** per tape plus **$3** per order for shipping and handling. (If you purchase 6-20 videos, the price is only **$14.95** each.)

Please send me ____ Youth on Board t-shirts for **$12** per shirt plus **$3** per order shipping and handling.

For large orders, call Youth on Board at 617/623-9900 x1242 for pricing information.

Name _____

Organization _____

Phone_____

Address _____

_____

City _____ State _____ Zip _____

Total Enclosed $ _____

Payment Method: ☐ Check (enclosed)   ☐ Visa   ☐ MasterCard

Card #_____ Expires_____

Signature _____

Make checks payable to **Youth on Board/YouthBuild USA** and mail to us at
58 Day Street, P.O. Box 440322, Somerville, MA 02144